CONTENTS

GET SOCIAL WITH US!

LIKE US: facebook.com/tasteofhome | **PIN US:** pinterest.com/taste_of_home

FOLLOW US: @tasteofhome | **TWEET US:** twitter.com/tasteofhome

TO FIND A RECIPE:
tasteofhome.com

**TO SUBMIT
A RECIPE:**
tasteofhome.com/
submit

**TO FIND OUT ABOUT
OTHER** *TASTE OF HOME*
PRODUCTS:
shoptasteofhome.com

INSTANT POT® 101

Let's get cooking! It's a snap to simmer a winner any night of the week when you have the right recipe and an Instant Pot at the ready. These popular devices are a great way for today's cooks to prepare delicious meals quickly and conveniently. Take a moment to review the next few pages so you can use yours like a pro.

WHAT IS AN INSTANT POT?
The term has become synonymous with pressure cooking—specifically, electric pressure cooking. But Instant Pot is actually a brand name for a popular electric pressure cooker, an airtight pot that cooks food quickly using steam pressure. When it comes to selecting an electric pressure cooker, there are several brands and sizes to choose from.

PICK YOUR POT
When determining the best device for you, consider how many people you cook for. This will help narrow the selection to the cooker that's the right size for your needs. Next, think about the features various models offer. For example: Is a yogurt-making option something you'd use regularly?

GET TO KNOW THE DESIGN
Electric pressure cookers have a lid that forms an airtight seal to create pressure; an inner pot that holds the food; and an outer pot with a control panel. For the most part, the buttons on the control panel are to help you set a cooking time. For example, if there is a "fish" button, pressing it will likely mean your food will cook for a short time (5 minutes or so). Some electric pressure cookers have a saute feature and others even offer a sterilize function. Most also include a slow-cook option, which allows you to cook your food slowly instead of pressure-cooking it.

THE PRESSURE'S ON
No matter what cooker you're using, you'll need to learn how to release the pressure safely. Because the escaping steam is hot enough to burn you, it's imperative you read and understand the directions that come with your pot for releasing pressure. Generally speaking, you'll either use a quick-release method (which involves pressing a handle or button) or the natural-release method (where the cooker cools down and releases pressure naturally). Always make sure the hole on top of the steam release is facing away from you before pressing the release button. And remember that the quick-release method is not suitable for soups (or anything with a large liquid volume) and cereals (or any dish with a high starch content), because quick-release may cause food to splatter out with the steam.

KEEP IT CLEAN
Follow the manufacturer's directions for cleaning your electric pressure cooker and review the tips and ideas on page 8, and you'll be cooking with it for years to come.

Taste *of* Home®
INSTANT POT®
COOKBOOK

DINNER IN AN INSTANT!

TASTE OF HOME BOOKS • RDA ENTHUSIAST BRANDS, LLC • MILWAUKEE, WI

Taste*of*Home

© 2018 RDA Enthusiast Brands, LLC.
1610 N. 2nd St., Suite 102, Milwaukee WI 53212-3906

Visit us at *tasteofhome.com* for other *Taste of Home* books and products.

INTERNATIONAL STANDARD BOOK NUMBER:
HARDCOVER: 978-1-61765-816-7
PAPERBACK: 978-1-61765-766-5

LIBRARY OF CONGRESS CONTROL NUMBER: 2018947083

COVER PHOTOGRAPHER: Dan Roberts

SET STYLIST: Dee Dee Schaefer

FOOD STYLIST: Sue Draheim

PICTURED ON FRONT COVER: Shredded Beef Burritos, p. 166

PICTURED ON BACK COVER: Cheddar Bacon Beer Dip, p. 22; Turkey with Berry Compote, p. 115; Edamame Salad with Sesame Seed Ginger Dressing, p. 213; Very Vanilla Cheesecake, p. 195

Printed in China

3 5 7 9 10 8 6 4

GET THE MOST OUT OF YOUR INSTANT POT®

Today's home cooks are turning to Instant Pots for everything from appetizers to desserts. But are they getting the ultimate out of these incredible kitchen helpers? Review these handy tips and see how you can save even more time and effort when using your Instant Pot.

LEARN HOW TO BOIL WATER (SERIOUSLY)

As soon as you get your cooker, start out by leaning how to boil water in it. Pour about 1 cup of water into the inner pot so you'll gain a sense of where the maximum fill line is. Seal the lid and select a short cook time. Within 5 minutes, the water should heat up and build pressure, at which point the pressure will release naturally. This is also a good time way to learn how to use the quick-release method.

TRY THE RICE COOKER FUNCTION

You can use your pot as a rice cooker. It takes about the same amount of time as cooking on the stovetop, with walk-away convenience, easy cleanup, and perfect results every time.

USE IT AS A STEAMER

Looking for a side of steamed veggies? Don't forget that these devices make great steamers. You can even use your Instant Pot to steam hard-boiled eggs—and you won't believe how easy they are to peel.

UP YOUR GAME WITH THE SAUTE FUNCTION

This is the one of the reasons people love Instant Pots. The saute function browns meats in the inner pot without dirtying a pan on the stovetop. You can also use this function on the low setting to simmer foods. This means you can simmer stock or beans after pressure-cooking them. And that means you can make soups and stews in a snap—all in one pot.

SAVE TIME WITH QUICK-RELEASE

To save time, let the pot cool down slightly, then manually release the pressure. The steam will be very hot, so be careful when moving the release to vent. A cool, wet towel placed on the lid can help speed up the release. Read the release directions that came with your cooker.

The best way to make the most of all-in-one cookers is to first understand what they can do and how they can save you time. A little bit of know-how goes a long way! Turn the page for more tips and hints on using your device.

HOW PRESSURE-COOKING WORKS

Pressure cookers build up hot steam and raise the pressure and temperature to simulate long braising, boiling or simmering. The resulting flavor is just as terrific as if you stood and stirred a bubbling pot all day.

LEARN THE BEST PRACTICES

Using a multipurpose cooker requires some reading and practice, so be patient. It will definitely be worth it in the end. Keep these hints in mind when using your cooker.

- Read the instruction manual that came with your electric pressure cooker before you make anything. Not all brands and models are the same, so get to know your pot!

- For food safety and efficiency, the total amount of food and liquid should never exceed the maximum level (also known as the max line or the fill line) indicated in the pot.

- Make sure the steam release valve is closed before you start cooking. Even the pros at the *Taste of Home* Test Kitchen have forgotten to close the valve and returned to see the pot venting instead of building pressure.

- The steam release valve is supposed to feel loose to the touch. The steam release handle works by simply applying pressure on the steam release pipe. Since the contact between the handle and the pipe is not fully sealed, the valve may release a little bit of steam while the food cooks.

- The power cord on some models is removable, which makes the appliance easier to store. If you plug it in and the light doesn't go on, check the cord. Is it attached securely? When the cooker isn't in use, consider storing the cord in the inner pot.

- After each use, remove and clean the rubber sealing ring, steam release valve and anti-block shield. See pages 8 and 9 for more on cleaning your electric pressure cooker.

- If your pot starts to smell like food even after cleaning it, put the sealing ring through the dishwasher. If that doesn't work, try steam cleaning: Pour 2 cups water and 1 Tbsp. lemon zest into the inner pot. Place the lid and run the steam program for 2 minutes. Carefully remove the sealing ring and let it air dry.

- Consider purchasing a separate sealing ring, using one for savory foods and one for sweet treats or foods with delicate flavors.

ARE YOU PLUGGED IN?

STORE CORD IN POT

TO CLEAN, REMOVE RUBBER SEALING RING

SNAP SEAL BACK

FAMILY COOKS SHARE THEIR BEST INSTANT POT® SECRETS

We asked Instant Pot fans to share their favorite hints and tips. Here's how they get the most out of an all-in-one cooker.

THINK BEFORE YOU COOK.
Before you begin cooking, determine if using the Instant Pot is the best method for the job. Not every dish is faster with the Instant Pot; however, the appliance will almost always save you active time. Instead of supervising the entree, you can be playing outside with the kids, relaxing or whipping up a yummy dessert while the main dish simmers.

HIT THE SAUTE FUNCTION EARLY.
Preheating your electric pressure cooker saves valuable time, so turn on the saute function while you prepare the ingredients. Slice and dice your veggies, and your Instant Pot will be ready to pressure-cook when you're finished.

CALCULATE PASTA'S COOK TIME.
Check the time your pasta package gives for cooking noodles in boiling water to al dente. Halve that time for Instant Pot cooking.

SUBSTITUTE BROWN RICE.
To substitute brown rice for regular white long grain, try increasing the cooking liquid by ¼ cup and the cook time by 5 minutes.

ADD THICKENER TO GRAVY.
Because there's no evaporation when you cook with an Instant Pot, braised recipes may have excess liquid. Try bumping up the cornstarch or flour a bit when adapting such recipes to all-in-one cookers.

TRY THESE "HARD-BOILED" EGGS.
Crack a few eggs into a baking dish, then pour a cup of water into your Instant Pot. Set the dish on the steamer rack inside the Instant Pot and pressure-cook on high for 5 minutes. When done, chop up the "egg loaf" for a head start on egg salad.

TURN THE HANDLES INTO LID HOLDERS.
The newer models' lid handles do double duty, holding the Instant Pot open with the lid out of the way. This feature is great for the buffet line. You also can store your Instant Pot this way to ensure the inside fully dries.

LET YOUR INSTANT POT® SHINE

Millions of home cooks have fallen in love with the Instant Pot; maybe you're one of them! If you love something, you need to take care of it. In the case of your all-in-one cooker, that means cleaning and drying it properly each and every time you use it.

Always unplug the device before washing. With the exception of the exterior cooker, or outer pot, all of the Instant Pot's parts are dishwasher safe, making life even easier.

You can allow the parts to dry in the dishwasher, or dry them by hand. Be sure everything, particularly the sealing ring, is completely dry before reassembling and storing.

See the pointers at right for even more washing and cleaning strategies.

WHAT TO WASH AFTER EVERY USE

INNER POT: The inner pot is made of stainless steel, so you can wash it in warm, soapy water or set it in the dishwasher. Since the food touches the pot directly, you'll definitely need to wash this pot after every use.

STEAM RACK: Since the steam rack sits in the inner pot and makes direct contact with the food, you'll need to wash this each time you cook with it. The rack will easily fit in the dishwasher, but feel free to wash by hand and dry completely.

STEAM RELEASE VALVE AND FLOAT VALVE: It's important to wipe food particles off these valves. You don't want anything blocking them, because that would hinder the steam from releasing when you are cooking future meals.

ANTI-BLOCK SHIELD: This is something that many cooks forget. Remove the shield from the lid. After hand washing it, wipe it with a soft cloth and dry completely. Make sure to secure it in place on the lid before using the appliance again.

SEALING RING: The sealing ring can absorb food odors, so you'll want to clean this after every use. Wash it by hand or toss it in the dishwasher. Make sure it's completely dry before setting it back on the lid. The ring is key to sealing the lid onto the pot and building pressure.

WHAT TO WASH OCCASIONALLY

EXTERIOR: Wipe the exterior of your Instant Pot with a damp cloth as needed. It's important not to submerge the cooker in water since it contains the heating element. When you need to clean the inside of the cooker (not to be confused with the inner pot), use a damp cloth.

LID: After carefully removing the sealing ring and the anti-block shield, wash the lid on the top rack of your dishwasher. It is not necessary to clean the lid after every use, but it's not a bad idea to simply give it a good wipe down with a clean kitchen towel or cotton cloth in between washes.

CONDENSATION CUP: This little cup collects the moisture that's created during the cooling process. It doesn't get particularly dirty, so a periodic wash is all it needs. You should check the cup regularly, however, and keep it clean with a quick wipedown every now and again.

DEEP-CLEANING BASICS

Show your Instant Pot some extra attention by giving it a deep clean every so often.

INNER POT: To refresh the inner pot, pour 1 cup of white vinegar into it and let sit for 5 minutes. Pour the vinegar out and rinse. If you start to see water stains, use a nonabrasive scouring cleanser to remove them.

SEALING RING: Give the ring a deep clean by adding 2 cups white vinegar and 1 tablespoon lemon zest to the inner pot and running the steam program for 2 minutes. Remove the sealing ring and let it air dry completely.

SNACKS & APPETIZERS

Take the stress out of hosting a party and let your multicooker do the work. Not only will you fill the buffet quickly, you'll keep the kitchen cool, free up oven space and have plenty of time to get your mingle on!

HOISIN MEATBALLS

Who doesn't love meatballs at a party? They're filling, comforting and hearty—great for summer fun and fall tailgates. In fact, the first time I served these savory bites was for our favorite team's opener. My best friend, who hates meatballs, couldn't get enough of them. I created a meatball convert. Woo-hoo! If you are serving children and prefer not to add the wine, simply substitute beef broth instead.
—Lisa de Perio, Dallas, TX

Prep: 20 min.
Cook: 10 min.
Makes: about 2 dozen

- 1 **cup dry red wine or beef broth**
- 3 **Tbsp. hoisin sauce**
- 2 **Tbsp. soy sauce**
- 1 **large egg, lightly beaten**
- 4 **green onions, chopped**
- ¼ **cup finely chopped onion**
- ¼ **cup minced fresh cilantro**
- 2 **garlic cloves, minced**
- ½ **tsp. salt**
- ½ **tsp. pepper**
- 1 **lb. ground beef**
- 1 **lb. ground pork**
  Sesame seeds

1. In a 6-qt. electric pressure cooker, whisk together wine, hoisin sauce and soy sauce. Bring to a boil. Reduce heat; simmer until liquid is reduced slightly.

2. In a large bowl, combine next seven ingredients. Add beef and pork; mix lightly but thoroughly. Shape into 1½-in. meatballs; place in cooker. Lock lid; make sure vent is closed. Select manual setting; adjust pressure to high, and set time for 10 minutes.

3. When finished cooking, quick-release pressure according to manufacturer's directions. Sprinkle with sesame seeds.

FREEZE OPTION: Freeze cooled meatballs in freezer containers. To use, partially thaw in refrigerator overnight. Microwave, covered, on high until heated through, about 8 minutes, gently stirring halfway through.

1 MEATBALL: 78 cal., 5g fat (2g sat. fat), 28mg chol., 156mg sod., 1g carb. (1g sugars, 0 fiber), 6g pro.

TEST KITCHEN TIP
Lighten things up a bit by using ground chicken or turkey in place of the ground beef.

CARIBBEAN CHIPOTLE PORK SLIDERS

One of our favorite pulled pork recipes combines the heat of chipotle peppers with cool tropical coleslaw. The robust flavors make these sliders a big hit with guests.
—Kadija Bridgewater, Boca Raton, FL

Prep: 35 min.
Cook: 75 min. + releasing
Makes: 20 servings

- 1 large onion, quartered
- 1 (3 to 4 lb.) boneless pork shoulder butt roast
- 2 chipotle peppers in adobo sauce, finely chopped
- 3 Tbsp. adobo sauce
- ¾ cup honey barbecue sauce
- ¼ cup water
- 4 garlic cloves, minced
- 1 Tbsp. ground cumin
- 1 tsp. salt
- ¼ tsp. pepper

COLESLAW

- 2 cups red cabbage, finely chopped
- 1 medium mango, peeled and chopped
- 1 cup pineapple tidbits, drained
- ¾ cup chopped fresh cilantro
- 1 Tbsp. lime juice
- ¼ tsp. salt
- ⅛ tsp. pepper
- 20 Hawaiian sweet rolls, split and toasted

1. Place onion in a 6-qt. electric pressure cooker. Cut roast in half; place over onion. In a small bowl, combine chipotle peppers, adobo sauce, barbecue sauce, water, garlic, cumin, salt and pepper; pour over meat. Lock lid; make sure vent is closed. Select manual; adjust pressure to high and set time for 75 minutes. When finished cooking, allow pressure to naturally release for 10 minutes and then quick-release any remaining pressure according to manufacturer's instructions.

2. Remove roast; cool slightly. Skim fat from cooking juices. If desired, select saute setting, and adjust for high heat. Cook the juices until slightly thickened.

3. Shred pork with two forks. Return pork to pressure cooker; stir to heat through.

4. For coleslaw, in a large bowl, combine cabbage, mango, pineapple, cilantro, lime juice, salt and pepper. Place ¼ cup pork mixture on each roll bottom; top with 2 Tbsp. coleslaw. Replace tops.

1 SLIDER: 265 cal., 10g fat (4g sat. fat), 55mg chol., 430mg sod., 27g carb. (15g sugars, 2g fiber), 16g pro.

CRANBERRY HOT WINGS

My daughter and her friends can't get enough of these cranberry-flavored wings. The popular appetizers remind me of all the wonderful celebrations and parties we've had through the years.
—Noreen McCormick Danek, Cromwell, CT

Prep: 45 min.
Cook: 35 min. + broiling
Makes: about 4 dozen

- 1 can (14 oz.) jellied cranberry sauce
- ½ cup orange juice
- ¼ cup hot pepper sauce
- 2 Tbsp. soy sauce
- 2 Tbsp. honey
- 1 Tbsp. brown sugar
- 1 Tbsp. Dijon mustard
- 2 tsp. garlic powder
- 1 tsp. dried minced onion
- 1 garlic clove, minced
- 5 lbs. chicken wings (about 24 wings)
- 1 tsp. salt
- 4 tsp. cornstarch
- 2 Tbsp. cold water

1. Whisk together first 10 ingredients. For chicken, use a sharp knife to cut through two wing joints; discard wing tips. Place wing pieces in a 6-qt. electric pressure cooker; sprinkle with salt. Pour cranberry mixture over top. Lock lid; make sure vent is closed. Select manual setting; adjust pressure to high, and set time for 10 minutes. When finished cooking, quick-release pressure according to manufacturer's directions.

2. Remove wings to a 15x10x1-in. pan; arrange in a single layer. Preheat broiler. Meanwhile, skim fat from cooking juices in pressure cooker. Select saute setting, and adjust for high heat. Bring juices to a boil; cook, stirring occasionally, until mixture is reduced by half, 20-25 minutes. In a small bowl, mix cornstarch and water until smooth; stir into juices. Return to a boil, stirring constantly; cook and stir until glaze is thickened, 1-2 minutes.

3. Broil wings 3-4 in. from heat until lightly browned, 2-3 minutes. Brush with glaze before serving. Serve with remaining glaze.

NOTE: Uncooked chicken wing sections (wingettes) may be substituted for whole chicken wings.

1 PIECE: 71 cal., 4g fat (1g sat. fat), 15mg chol., 122mg sod., 5g carb. (3g sugars, 0 fiber), 5g pro.

GARLIC-DILL DEVILED EGGS

I like to experiment with my recipes and was pleasantly surprised with how fresh dill perked up the flavor of these irresistible party classics.
—Kami Horch, Calais, ME

Prep: 20 min. + chilling
Cook: 5 min. + releasing
Makes: 2 dozen

- 1 **cup cold water**
- 12 **large eggs**
- ⅔ **cup mayonnaise**
- 4 **tsp. dill pickle relish**
- 2 **tsp. snipped fresh dill**
- 2 **tsp. Dijon mustard**
- 1 **tsp. coarsely ground pepper**
- ¼ **tsp. garlic powder**
- ⅛ **tsp. paprika or cayenne pepper**

1. Pour water into 6-qt. electric pressure cooker. Place trivet in cooker; set eggs on trivet. Lock lid; make sure vent is closed. Select manual setting; adjust pressure to low, and set time to 4 minutes. When finished cooking, allow pressure to naturally release for 5 minutes; quick-release any remaining pressure according to manufacturer's directions. Immediately place eggs in a bowl of ice water to cool.

2. Cut eggs lengthwise in half. Remove yolks, reserving the whites. In a bowl, mash yolks. Stir in all remaining ingredients except paprika. Spoon or pipe into egg whites.

3. Refrigerate, covered, at least 30 minutes before serving. Sprinkle with paprika.

1 STUFFED EGG HALF: 78 cal., 7g fat (1g sat. fat), 93mg chol., 86mg sod., 1g carb. (0 sugars, 0 fiber), 3g pro.

PORK PICADILLO LETTUCE WRAPS

Warm pork and cool, crisp lettuce are a combination born in culinary heaven. My spin on a first-course lettuce wrap is loaded with flavor and spice.
—Janice Elder, Charlotte, NC

Prep: 30 min.
Cook: 25 min. + releasing
Makes: 2 dozen

- 3 garlic cloves, minced
- 1 Tbsp. chili powder
- 1 tsp. salt
- ½ tsp. pumpkin pie spice
- ½ tsp. ground cumin
- ½ tsp. pepper
- 2 pork tenderloins (1 lb. each)
- 1 large onion, chopped
- 1 small Granny Smith apple, peeled and chopped
- 1 small sweet red pepper, chopped
- 1 can (10 oz.) diced tomatoes and green chilies, undrained
- 1 cup water
- ½ cup golden raisins
- ½ cup chopped pimiento-stuffed olives
- 24 Bibb or Boston lettuce leaves
- ¼ cup slivered almonds, toasted

1. Mix garlic and seasonings; rub over pork. Transfer to a 6-qt. electric pressure cooker. Add onion, apple, sweet pepper, tomatoes and water. Lock lid; make sure vent is closed. Select manual setting; adjust pressure to high and set time for 25 minutes. When finished cooking, allow pressure to naturally release for 10 minutes and then quick-release any remaining pressure according to manufacturer's instructions.

2. Remove pork; cool slightly. Shred meat into bite-size pieces; return to pressure cooker.

3. Select saute setting and adjust for low heat. Stir in raisins and olives; heat through. Serve in lettuce leaves; sprinkle with slivered almonds.

1 WRAP: 75 cal., 3g fat (1g sat. fat), 21mg chol., 232mg sod., 5g carb. (3g sugars, 1g fiber), 8g pro.

CHEDDAR BACON BEER DIP

My tangy, smoky dip won the top prize at our office party recipe contest. Use whatever beer you like, but steer clear of particularly dark varieties.
—Ashley Lecker, Green Bay, WI

Prep: 15 min.
Cook: 10 min.
Makes: 4½ cups

18 oz. cream cheese, softened
¼ cup sour cream
1½ Tbsp. Dijon mustard
1 tsp. garlic powder
1 cup beer or nonalcoholic beer
1 lb. bacon strips, cooked and crumbled
2 cups shredded cheddar cheese
¼ cup heavy whipping cream
1 green onion, thinly sliced
Soft pretzel bites

1. In a greased 6-qt. electric pressure cooker, combine cream cheese, sour cream, mustard and garlic powder until smooth. Stir in beer; add crumbled bacon, reserving 2 Tbsp. Lock lid; make sure vent is closed. Select manual setting; adjust pressure to high, and set time for 5 minutes. When finished cooking, quick-release pressure according to manufacturer's directions.

2. Select saute setting, and adjust for normal heat. Stir in cheese and heavy cream. Cook and stir until mixture has thickened, 3-4 minutes. Transfer to serving dish. Sprinkle with onion and reserved bacon. Serve with pretzel bites.

¼ **CUP:** 213 cal., 19g fat (10g sat. fat), 60mg chol., 378mg sod., 2g carb. (1g sugars, 0 fiber), 8g pro.

TEST KITCHEN TIP
Your favorite ale will also work in this recipe. Our Test Kitchen staff loved the flavor of New Belgium Fat Tire.

APPLE-PEAR COMPOTE

Sweeten up snack time with this comforting compote. Spread the apple-pear mixture on pieces of pound cake, toasted English muffins, shortbread cookies or even crackers. You can also enjoy the compote on its own with a bit of whipped cream. I sometimes add raisins or chopped nuts to the compote, and for a more adult flavor I add ⅓ cup brandy or rum.
—Nancy Heishman, Las Vegas, NV

Prep: 20 min.
Cook: 10 min. + releasing
Makes: 8 cups

- 5 **medium apples, peeled and chopped**
- 3 **medium pears, chopped**
- 1 **medium orange, thinly sliced**
- ½ **cup dried cranberries**
- ½ **cup packed brown sugar**
- ½ **cup maple syrup**
- ⅓ **cup butter, cubed**
- 2 **Tbsp. lemon juice**
- 2 **tsp. ground cinnamon**
- 1 **tsp. ground ginger**
- 5 **Tbsp. orange juice, divided**
- 4 **tsp. cornstarch**

1. In a 6-qt. electric pressure cooker, combine the first 10 ingredients. Stir in 2 Tbsp. orange juice. Lock lid; make sure vent is closed. Select manual setting; adjust pressure to high and set time for 6 minutes. When finished cooking, allow pressure to naturally release for 5 minutes and then quick-release any remaining pressure according to manufacturer's instructions.

2. Select saute setting and adjust for high heat; bring liquid to a boil. In a small bowl, mix cornstarch and remaining orange juice until smooth; gradually stir into fruit mixture. Cook and stir until sauce is thickened, 1 to 2 minutes.

½ **CUP:** 149 cal., 4g fat (2g sat. fat), 10mg chol., 34mg sod., 30g carb. (25g sugars, 2g fiber), 0 pro.

BREAKFAST & BRUNCH

Turn here for impressive eye-openers that cook up fast. From busy weekday mornings to Sunday get-togethers, the perfect recipe is at your fingertips.

COZY FRUIT COMPOTE

You can prepare this colorful and easy fruit relish up to a week in advance, so it's handy whenever you need a sweet topper. It's a tasty addition to brunch lineups.
—Esther Chesney, Carthage, MO

Takes: 10 min. + releasing
Makes: 2½ cups

- 1 pkg. (12 oz.) fresh or 3 cups frozen cranberries
- ⅔ cup packed brown sugar
- ¼ cup thawed orange juice concentrate
- 2 Tbsp. raspberry vinegar
- ½ cup chopped dried apricots
- ½ cup golden raisins
- ½ cup chopped walnuts, toasted

1. In a 6-qt. electric pressure cooker, combine cranberries, brown sugar, orange juice concentrate and vinegar. Lock lid; make sure vent is closed. Select manual setting; adjust pressure to high, and set time for 3 minutes. When finished cooking, allow pressure to naturally release for 5 minutes, then quick-release any remaining pressure according to manufacturer's directions.

2. Stir in apricots, raisins and walnuts. Refrigerate leftovers.

2 TBSP.: 161 cal., 4g fat (0 sat. fat), 0 chol., 32mg sod., 32g carb. (28g sugars, 3g fiber), 2g pro.

TEST KITCHEN TIP
This compote is delightful over waffles, pancakes and French toast, but try it alongside cooked pork, chicken and turkey as well.

PUMPKIN SPICE OATMEAL

There's nothing like a bowl of warm oatmeal in the morning, and my spiced version works in an electric pressure cooker. Be sure to store leftovers in the fridge.
—Jordan Mason, Brookville, PA

Takes: 20 min. + releasing
Makes: 6 servings

1¼ cups steel-cut oats
3 Tbsp. brown sugar
1½ tsp. pumpkin pie spice
1 tsp. ground cinnamon
¾ tsp. salt
3 cups water
1½ cups 2% milk
1 can (15 oz.) solid-pack pumpkin
 Optional toppings: toasted chopped pecans, ground cinnamon, additional brown sugar and 2% milk

1. Stir together first seven ingredients in a 6-qt. electric pressure cooker. Lock lid; make sure vent is closed. Select manual setting; adjust pressure to high and set time for 10 minutes.

2. When finished cooking, allow pressure to naturally release for 10 minutes, then quick-release any remaining pressure according to manufacturer's directions. Stir in pumpkin; let stand 5-10 minutes to thicken. Serve with toppings as desired.

NOTE: Steel-cut oats are also known as Scotch oats or Irish oatmeal.

1 CUP: 208 cal., 4g fat (1g sat. fat), 5mg chol., 329mg sod., 39g carb. (13g sugars, 6g fiber), 7g pro.

TEST KITCHEN TIP
To turn this recipe into gingerbread oatmeal, replace half the brown sugar with molasses and sprinkle oatmeal with a little candied ginger before serving.

HAM & CHEDDAR BREAKFAST CASSEROLE

This cheesy casserole has made appearances at holiday breakfasts, potlucks and even my daughter's college apartment to feed her hungry roommates. It's my go-to recipe for any action-packed morning.
—Patty Bernhard, Greenville, OH

Prep: 20 min.
Cook: 35 min. + releasing
Makes: 6 servings

6 large eggs
½ cup 2% milk
½ tsp. salt
¼ tsp. pepper
4 cups frozen shredded hash brown potatoes, thawed
1 cup cubed fully cooked ham
½ medium onion, chopped
2 cups shredded cheddar cheese
1 cup water

1. Whisk together eggs, milk, salt and pepper. Combine the potatoes, ham, onion and cheese; transfer to a greased 2-qt. souffle or round baking dish; pour egg mixture over top.

2. Pour water into a 6-qt. electric pressure cooker. Cover baking dish with foil. Place on a trivet with handles; lower into pressure cooker. Lock lid; make sure vent is closed.

3. Select manual setting; adjust pressure to high, and set time for 35 minutes. When finished cooking, allow pressure to naturally release for 10 minutes, then quick-release any remaining pressure according to manufacturer's directions. Let stand 10 minutes before serving.

1 SERVING: 324 cal., 19g fat (9g sat. fat), 239mg chol., 17mg sod., 17g carb. (3g sugars, 1g fiber), 22g pro.

TEST KITCHEN TIP
Other cooked breakfast meats, including turkey or pork sausage and bacon crumbles, will work well in this recipe.

SUNDAY BRUNCH BROCCOLI EGG CUPS

Serving brunch for a few friends? This delicious egg bake is filled with crunchy bites of broccoli and served in ramekins. I promise your guests will love it!
—Edna Hoffman, Hebron, IN

Takes: 25 min.
Makes: 4 servings

- 7 **large eggs**
- 1½ **cups half-and-half cream**
- 3 **Tbsp. shredded Swiss cheese**
- 2 **tsp. minced fresh parsley**
- 1 **tsp. minced fresh basil**
- ¼ **tsp. salt**
- ⅛ **tsp. cayenne pepper**
- 1 **to 1½ cups frozen broccoli florets, thawed**
- 1 **cup water**

1. Whisk three eggs with next six ingredients; pour into four greased 8-oz. ramekins. Divide broccoli among ramekins; top each with one remaining egg.

2. Add 1 cup water and trivet insert to a 6-qt. electric pressure cooker. Place ramekins on trivet, offset-stacking as needed, and covering loosely with foil. Lock lid; make sure vent is closed. Select steam setting; adjust pressure to high, and set time for 6 minutes. When finished cooking, quick-release pressure according to manufacturers' directions. Remove lid; using tongs, carefully remove the ramekins. Let stand for 3 minutes before serving.

1 SERVING: 274 cal., 19g fat (10g sat. fat), 375mg chol., 333mg sod., 5g carb. (4g sugars, 1g fiber), 16g pro.

NUTTY APPLE BUTTER

Grab some apples and peanut butter to make this creamy change-of-pace spread. We use it with sliced fruit or graham crackers, and we even spread it on sandwiches.
—Brandie Cranshaw, Rapid City, SD

Prep: 20 min.
Cook: 3 min. + releasing
Makes: 5 cups

- 4 **lbs. (about 8) large apples, cored and quartered**
- ¾ **to 1 cup sugar**
- ¼ **cup water**
- 3 **tsp. ground cinnamon**
- ¼ **tsp. ground nutmeg**
- ¼ **tsp. ground cloves**
- ¼ **tsp. ground allspice**
- ¼ **cup creamy peanut butter**

1. In a 6-qt. electric pressure cooker, combine the first seven ingredients. Lock lid; make sure vent is closed. Select manual setting; adjust pressure to high and set time for 3 minutes. When finished cooking, allow pressure to naturally release for 5 minutes and then quick-release any remaining pressure according to manufacturer's instructions.

2. Mash apples with a potato masher or use an immersion blender until blended. Whisk in peanut butter until apple mixture is smooth. Cool to room temperature. Store in airtight container in the refrigerator.

2 TBSP.: 43 cal., 1g fat (0 sat. fat), 0 chol., 9mg sod., 9g carb. (8g sugars, 1g fiber), 0 pro.

DENVER OMELET FRITTATA

Pepper, onion and ham go into this classic breakfast dish made simple. It's the perfect entree to enjoy after church or another early outing.
—Connie Eaton, Pittsburgh, PA

Prep: 25 min.
Cook: 35 min. + releasing
Makes: 6 servings

- 1 Tbsp. olive oil
- 1 medium Yukon Gold potato, peeled and sliced
- 1 small onion, thinly sliced
- 1 cup water
- 12 large eggs
- 1 tsp. hot pepper sauce
- ½ tsp. salt
- ¼ tsp. pepper
- 8 oz. sliced deli ham, chopped
- ½ cup chopped green pepper
- 1 cup shredded cheddar cheese, divided

1. Select saute setting on a 6-qt. electric pressure cooker and adjust for high heat; then heat oil. Add potato and onion; cook and stir 4-6 minutes or until potato is lightly browned. Transfer to a greased 1½ qt. (6- or 7-in.) souffle or round baking dish. Wipe pressure cooker clean. Pour in water.

2. In a large bowl, whisk eggs, pepper sauce, salt and pepper; stir in ham, green pepper and ½ cup cheese. Pour over potato mixture. Top with remaining cheese. Cover baking dish with foil and place on a trivet with handles; lower into pressure cooker. Lock lid; make sure vent is closed.

3. Select manual setting; adjust pressure to high and set time for 35 minutes. When finished cooking, allow pressure to naturally release for 10 minutes; quick-release any remaining pressure according to manufacturer's instructions.

1 WEDGE: 320 cal., 19g fat (7g sat. fat), 407mg chol., 822mg sod., 12g carb. (3g sugars, 1g fiber), 25g pro.

CHERRY-ALMOND OATMEAL

If you're craving a sweet and satisfying breakfast, try my hot cereal. It's so simple...just place the ingredients in the pressure cooker and then treat yourself to a comforting bowl of goodness.
—Geraldine Saucier, Albuquerque, NM

Prep: 10 min.
Cook: 12 min. + releasing
Makes: 6 servings

- 4 **cups vanilla almond milk**
- 1 **cup steel-cut oats**
- 1 **cup dried cherries**
- ⅓ **cup packed brown sugar**
- ½ **tsp. salt**
- ½ **tsp. ground cinnamon**
  Additional vanilla almond milk, optional

In a 6-qt. electric pressure cooker coated with cooking spray, combine first 6 ingredients. Lock lid; make sure vent is closed. Select manual setting; adjust pressure to high and set time for 12 minutes. When finished cooking, allow pressure to naturally release for 10 minutes; quick-release any remaining pressure according to manufacturer's instructions. Serve with additional almond milk if desired.

1 SERVING: 276 cal., 4g fat (0 sat. fat), 0 chol., 57mg sod., 57g carb. (35g sugars, 4g fiber), 5g pro.

WHY YOU'LL LOVE IT...

"We loved this breakfast. It was quick and easy to put together; definitely a keeper!"
—ARISACUPP, TASTEOFHOME.COM

FRITTATA PROVENCAL

This meatless dish makes a savory brunch for lazy weekend mornings, but I like it so much that I enjoy it for dinner during the week, too.
—Connie Eaton, Pittsburgh, PA

Prep: 30 min.
Cook: 35 min. + releasing
Makes: 6 servings

- 1 Tbsp. olive oil
- 1 medium Yukon Gold potato, peeled and sliced
- 1 small onion, thinly sliced
- ½ tsp. smoked paprika
- 1 cup water
- 12 large eggs
- 1 tsp. minced fresh thyme or ¼ tsp. dried thyme
- 1 tsp. hot pepper sauce
- ½ tsp. salt
- ¼ tsp. pepper
- 1 log (4 oz.) crumbled fresh goat cheese, divided
- ½ cup chopped sun-dried tomatoes (not packed in oil)

1. Select saute setting on a 6-qt. electric pressure cooker; adjust for high heat. Then heat oil. Add potato and onion; cook and stir until potato is lightly browned, 5-7 minutes. Stir in paprika. Transfer potato mixture to a greased 1½-qt. souffle or round baking dish. Wipe pressure cooker clean. Pour in water.

2. In a large bowl, whisk next five ingredients; stir in 2 oz. cheese. Pour over potato mixture. Top with tomatoes and remaining goat cheese. Cover baking dish with foil; place on a trivet with handles. Lower into pressure cooker. Lock lid; make sure vent is closed.

3. Select manual setting; adjust pressure to high, and set time for 35 minutes. When finished cooking, allow pressure to naturally release for 10 minutes, then quick-release any remaining pressure according to manufacturer's directions.

1 SERVING: 245 cal., 14g fat (5g sat. fat), 385mg chol., 12mg sod., 12g carb. (4g sugars, 2g fiber), 15g pro.

TEST KITCHEN TIP
Smoked paprika adds a rich flavor to this breakfast entree. Use it as a replacement for ground chipotle pepper in recipes, or simply add a pinch to chili and your other southwestern favorites.

SAUSAGE & WAFFLE BAKE

Here's an easy dish guaranteed to create excitement at the breakfast table! Nothing is missing from this sweet and savory combination. It's so wrong, it's right!
—Courtney Lentz, Boston, MA

Prep: 20 min.
Cook: 20 min. + releasing
Makes: 6 servings

- 1 **lb. bulk spicy breakfast pork sausage**
- 1½ **tsp. rubbed sage**
- ¼ **tsp. fennel seed**
- 5 **frozen waffles, cut into bite-sized pieces**
- 1 **cup water**
- 4 **large eggs**
- ⅔ **cup half-and-half cream**
- 2 **Tbsp. maple syrup**
- ⅛ **tsp. salt**
- ⅛ **tsp. pepper**
- 1 **cup shredded cheddar cheese**
  Additional maple syrup

1. Select saute setting on a 6-qt. electric pressure cooker and adjust for normal heat. Cook and crumble sausage; drain fat. Add sage and fennel. Place waffles in a greased 1½-qt. souffle or round (6- or 7-in.) baking dish; top with sausage. Wipe pressure cooker clean; pour in 1 cup water.

2. In a bowl, mix eggs, cream, syrup and seasonings. Pour over sausage and waffles. Top with cheese. Cover baking dish with foil; place on a trivet with handles. Lower into pressure cooker. Lock lid; make sure vent is closed.

3. Select manual setting; adjust pressure to high and set time for 20 minutes. When finished cooking, allow pressure to naturally release for 5 minutes and then quick-release any remaining pressure according to manufacturer's instructions. Serve with additional maple syrup.

1 SERVING: 445 cal., 31g fat (12g sat. fat), 201mg chol., 880mg sod., 20g carb. (7g sugars, 1g fiber), 19g pro.

POTATO-CHEDDAR FRITTATA

I like to serve this protein-packed frittata with toasted rustic bread. You can also use your own leftover potatoes instead of the prepackaged potatoes with onions.
—Donna Marie Ryan, Topsfield, MA

Prep: 15 min. + standing
Cook: 30 min. + releasing
Makes: 4 servings

- 1 Tbsp. canola oil
- 1½ cups refrigerated diced potatoes with onion
- 1 cup water
- 8 large egg whites
- 4 large eggs
- ½ cup fat-free milk
- 2 green onions, chopped
- 2 tsp. minced fresh parsley
- ¼ tsp. salt
- ¼ tsp. pepper
- ½ cup shredded cheddar cheese

1. In a large skillet, heat oil over medium-high heat. Add potatoes; cook and stir until lightly browned, 4-6 minutes. Transfer to a greased 1½ -2½ qt. souffle or round baking dish. Add 1 cup water and trivet insert for a 6-qt. electric pressure cooker.

2. Whisk next seven ingredients; stir in shredded cheese. Pour egg mixture over potatoes. Loosely cover baking dish with aluminum foil. Lock lid; make sure vent is closed. Select manual setting; adjust pressure to high, and set time to 30 minutes.

3. After cooking, let pressure release naturally for 10 minutes, then quick-release any remaining pressure according to manufacturer's directions. Remove baking dish. Let stand for 10 minutes.

1 WEDGE: 241 cal., 13g fat (5g sat. fat), 201mg chol., 555mg sod., 11g carb. (2g sugars, 1g fiber), 19g pro. **DIABETIC EXCHANGES:** 2 medium-fat meat, 1 starch, 1 fat.

CARROT CAKE OATMEAL

This warm breakfast cereal is a great way to get your veggies in the morning and keep a healthy diet! For extra crunch, I garnish individual servings with ground walnuts or pecans.
—Debbie Kain, Colorado Springs, CO

Prep: 10 min.
Cook: 10 min. + releasing
Makes: 8 servings

4½ cups water
1 can (20 oz.) crushed pineapple, undrained
2 cups shredded carrots
1 cup steel-cut oats
1 cup raisins
2 tsp. ground cinnamon
1 tsp. pumpkin pie spice
Brown sugar, optional

In a 6-qt. electric pressure cooker coated with cooking spray, combine the first seven ingredients. Lock lid; make sure vent is closed. Select manual setting; adjust pressure to high, and set time for 10 minutes. When finished cooking, allow pressure to naturally release for 10 minutes, then quick-release any remaining pressure according to manufacturer's directions. If desired, sprinkle with brown sugar.

1 SERVING: 197 cal., 2g fat (0 sat. fat), 0 chol., 46mg sod., 46g carb. (26g sugars, 4g fiber), 4g pro.

TEST KITCHEN TIP
Steel-cut oats are also known as Scotch oats or Irish oatmeal. You can find them near the other varieties of oats and oatmeal at your local grocery store.

SIDE DISHES

Leave the oven for the entrees and put your Instant Pot® to work with these savory menu additions. What could be easier, quicker or more delicious? Best of all, they travel well for potlucks and other bring-a-dish parties.

LORA'S RED BEANS & RICE

My mother-in-law passed this simple recipe to me. With meats, beans and savory veggies, it's tasty, easy and economical, too!
—Carol Simms, Madison, MS

Prep: 15 min. + soaking
Cook: 30 min.
Makes: 10 servings

1 **pkg. (16 oz.) dried kidney beans (about 2½ cups)**
2 **cups cubed fully cooked ham (about 1 lb.)**
1 **pkg. (12 oz.) fully cooked andouille chicken sausage links or flavor of choice, sliced**
1 **medium green pepper, chopped**
1 **medium onion, chopped**
2 **celery ribs, chopped**
1 **Tbsp. hot pepper sauce**
2 **garlic cloves, minced**
1½ **tsp. salt**
   Hot cooked rice

1. Rinse and sort beans. Soak overnight according to package directions. Drain, discarding water; rinse with cool water.

2. In a 6-qt. electric pressure cooker, combine ham, sausage, vegetables, pepper sauce, garlic, salt and enough water to cover (about 4 cups). Lock lid; make sure vent is closed. Select manual setting; adjust pressure to high, and set time for 30 minutes. When finished cooking, quick-release pressure according to manufacturer's directions. Serve with rice.

1 CUP BEAN MIXTURE: 249 cal., 5g fat (1g sat. fat), 43mg chol., 906mg sod., 31g carb. (2g sugars, 7g fiber), 23g pro.

ORANGE SPICE CARROTS

To get my son to eat veggies, I mix and match flavors and spices. Thank goodness my carrots with orange and cinnamon won him over. He can't get enough of them!
—Christina Addison, Blanchester, OH

Takes: 15 min.
Makes: 6 servings

- 2 lbs. medium carrots or baby carrots, cut into ¾-in. pieces
- ½ cup packed brown sugar
- ½ cup orange juice
- 2 Tbsp. butter
- ¾ tsp. ground cinnamon
- ½ tsp. salt
- ¼ tsp. ground nutmeg
- 1 Tbsp. cornstarch
- ¼ cup cold water

TEST KITCHEN TIP
For extra zing, top the colorful carrots with a little orange zest.

1. In a 6-qt. electric pressure cooker, combine the first seven ingredients. Lock lid; make sure vent is closed. Select manual setting; adjust pressure to low and set time for 3 minutes. When finished cooking, quick-release pressure according to manufacturer's directions.

2. Select saute setting, and adjust for high heat; bring liquid to a boil. In a small bowl, mix cornstarch and water until smooth; gradually stir into carrot mixture. Cook and stir until sauce is thickened, 1-2 minutes.

⅔ **CUP:** 187 cal., 4g fat (3g sat. fat), 10mg chol., 339mg sod., 38g carb. (27g sugars, 4g fiber), 2g pro.

TRULY TASTY TURNIP GREENS

These greens are a hit at every church dinner I take them to. Adjust the seasonings as you please to make the recipe all your own.
—Amy Inman, Hiddenite, NC

Prep: 20 min.
Cook: 5 min. + releasing
Makes: 14 servings

- 2 lbs. peeled turnips, cut into ½-in. cubes
- 12 oz. fresh turnip greens
- 8 oz. fully cooked country ham or 2 smoked ham hocks
- 1 medium onion, chopped
- 3 Tbsp. sugar
- 1½ tsp. coarsely ground pepper
- ¾ tsp. salt
- 2 cartons (32 oz. each) chicken broth

1. In a 6-qt. electric pressure cooker, combine all ingredients. Lock lid; make sure vent is closed. Select manual setting; adjust pressure to high, and set time for 5 minutes. When finished cooking, allow pressure to naturally release for 10 minutes, then quick-release any remaining pressure according to manufacturer's directions.

2. If using ham hocks, remove meat from bones when cool enough to handle; cut ham into small pieces and return to pressure cooker. Serve with a slotted spoon.

¾ CUP: 63 cal., 1g fat (0 sat. fat), 11mg chol., 903mg sod., 9g carb. (6g sugars, 2g fiber), 5g pro.

TEST KITCHEN TIP
Sugar is added to many recipes for turnip greens to offset their somewhat bitter flavor. Feel free to adjust the amount to suit your taste.

LEMON RED POTATOES

Butter, lemon juice, parsley and chives enhance this quick side dish. I usually prepare these potatoes when I'm having company. Since they cook in the mulitcooker, there's plenty of room on the stove for other items.
—Tara Branham, Austin, TX

Takes: 20 min.
Makes: 6 servings

1½ lbs. medium red
    potatoes
¼ cup water
¼ cup butter, melted
3 Tbsp. minced fresh
    parsley
1 Tbsp. lemon juice
1 Tbsp. minced chives
    Salt and pepper to taste

1. Cut a strip of peel around the middle of each potato. Place potatoes and water in a 6-qt. electric pressure cooker. Lock lid; make sure vent is closed. Select manual setting; adjust pressure to high and set time for 12 minutes. When finished cooking, quick-release pressure according to manufacturer's directions. Drain any cooking liquid; return potatoes to pressure cooker.

2. In a small bowl, combine butter, parsley, lemon juice and chives. Pour over the potatoes; toss to coat. Sprinkle with salt and pepper.

1 SERVING: 150 cal., 8g fat (5g sat. fat), 20mg chol., 85mg sod., 18g carb. (1g sugars, 2g fiber), 2g pro.

CELEBRATION BRUSSELS SPROUTS

This recipe hits all the flavor points and makes a fantastic side for special menus. Plus, you have to love a dish that requires minimal effort and doesn't take up oven space. You can always omit the bacon if you need a vegetarian option.
—Lauren Knoelke, Milwaukee, WI

Takes: 25 min.
Makes: 10 servings

- 2 lbs. fresh Brussels sprouts, sliced
- 2 large apples (Fuji or Braeburn), chopped
- ⅓ cup dried cranberries
- 8 bacon strips, cooked and crumbled, divided
- ⅓ cup cider vinegar
- ¼ cup maple syrup
- 2 Tbsp. olive oil
- 1 tsp. salt
- ½ tsp. coarsely ground pepper
- ¾ cup chopped hazelnuts or pecans, toasted

Combine Brussels sprouts, apples, cranberries and 4 slices bacon. In a small bowl, whisk vinegar, syrup, oil, salt and pepper; pour over Brussels sprouts mixture, tossing to coat. Transfer to a 6-qt. electric pressure cooker. Lock lid; make sure vent is closed. Select manual setting; adjust pressure to high and set time for 3 minutes. When finished cooking, quick-release pressure according to manufacturer's directions. To serve, sprinkle with hazelnuts and remaining bacon.

1 SERVING: 204 cal., 11g fat (2g sat. fat), 7mg chol., 375mg sod., 24g carb. (15g sugars, 5g fiber), 6g pro.

TEST KITCHEN TIP
When an Instant Pot® recipe calls for apples, Fujis or Braeburns are usually your best bet. They have a crisp texture that holds up to the intense heat during cooking.

SWEET & SOUR BEET SALAD

My husband loves pickled beets. I paired them with a little citrus for this change-of-pace salad. What a colorful (and flavorful) combo!
—Michelle Clair, Seattle, WA

Prep: 15 min.
Cook: 20 min.
Makes: 8 servings

- 6 **medium fresh beets (about 2 lbs.)**
- 1½ **cups water**
- ¼ **cup extra virgin olive oil**
- 3 **Tbsp. lemon juice**
- 2 **Tbsp. cider vinegar**
- 2 **Tbsp. honey**
- ¼ **tsp. salt**
- ¼ **tsp. pepper**
- 2 **large ruby red grapefruit, peeled and sectioned**
- 2 **small red onions, halved and thinly sliced**

1. Scrub beets, trimming tops to 1 in. Place beets on trivet of a 6-qt. electric pressure cooker. Add 1½ cups water. Lock lid; make sure vent is closed. Select manual setting; adjust pressure to high and set time to 20 minutes.

2. When finished cooking, let pressure release naturally before opening; remove beets and cool completely before peeling, halving and thinly slicing them. Place in a serving bowl. Whisk together next six ingredients. Pour over beets; add grapefruit and onion. Toss gently to coat.

¾ **CUP:** 161 cal., 7g fat (1g sat. fat), 0 chol., 162mg sod., 24g carb. (20g sugars, 4g fiber), 3g pro. **DIABETIC EXCHANGES:** 1½ fat, 1 starch, 1 vegetable.

CHEESY BACON SPAGHETTI SQUASH

This 30-minute casserole is called cheesy for a reason. We like it with Swiss, but you can stir in any kind you have in the fridge. Just don't skimp on the bacon!
—Jean Williams, Stillwater, OK

Takes: 30 min.
Makes: 4 servings

- 1 **large spaghetti squash (3½ lbs.)**
- 1 **cup water**
- 4 **bacon strips, chopped**
- 3 **Tbsp. butter**
- 1 **Tbsp. brown sugar**
- ½ **tsp. salt**
- ¼ **tsp. pepper**
- ½ **cup shredded Swiss cheese**

1. Halve squash lengthwise; discard seeds. Place squash, cut side down, on the trivet of a 6-qt. electric pressure cooker. Add water to cooker; insert trivet. Lock lid; make sure vent is closed. Select steam setting; adjust pressure to high and set time to 7 minutes. When finished cooking, quick-release pressure according to manufacturer's directions. Set aside; remove squash, trivet and water from cooker.

2. Select saute setting, and adjust for high heat; add bacon, stirring occasionally, and cook until crisp. With a slotted spoon, remove bacon to paper towels; reserve drippings. Stir in butter, brown sugar, salt and pepper. Separate squash strands with a fork and add to cooker; toss and heat through. Remove from heat. Stir in cheese, and place in a serving bowl. Top with bacon.

1 CUP: 383 cal., 26g fat (12g sat. fat), 54mg chol., 643mg sod., 31g carb. (4g sugars, 6g fiber), 10g pro.

BBQ BAKED BEANS

I was under doctor's orders to reduce the amount of sodium I was eating, but I just couldn't part with some of my favorite foods. After many experiments I came up with this potluck favorite—now everyone's happy!
—Sherrel Hendrix, Arkadelphia, AR

Prep: 10 min. + soaking
Cook: 35 min. + releasing
Makes: 12 servings

- 1 pkg. (16 oz.) dried great northern beans
- 2 smoked ham hocks (about ½ lb. each)
- 2 cups water
- 1 medium onion, chopped
- 2 tsp. garlic powder, divided
- 2 tsp. onion powder, divided
- 1 cup barbecue sauce
- ¾ cup packed brown sugar
- ½ tsp. ground nutmeg
- ¼ tsp. ground cloves
- 2 tsp. hot pepper sauce, optional

1. Rinse and sort beans; soak according to package directions. Drain and rinse beans, discarding liquid.

2. In a 6-qt. electric pressure cooker, combine beans, ham hocks, water, onion, 1 tsp. garlic powder and 1 tsp. onion powder. Lock lid; make sure vent is closed. Select manual setting; adjust pressure to high and set time for 30 minutes. When finished cooking, allow pressure to naturally release for 10 minutes, then quick-release any remaining pressure according to manufacturer's directions.

3. Remove ham hocks; cool slightly. Cut meat into small cubes, discarding bones; return meat to pressure cooker. Stir in barbecue sauce, brown sugar, nutmeg, cloves, remaining garlic powder, remaining onion powder and, if desired, hot pepper sauce. Lock lid; make sure vent is closed. Select manual setting; adjust pressure to high and set time for 3 minutes. When finished cooking, allow pressure to naturally release for 5 minutes, then quick-release any remaining pressure according to manufacturer's directions.

½ **CUP:** 238 cal., 1g fat (0 sat. fat), 4mg chol., 347mg sod., 48g carb. (22g sugars, 8g fiber), 10g pro.

TEST KITCHEN TIP
Watching your sodium? Using hot sauce to flavor foods can be a smart alternative to salt, but make sure you check the nutrition label. Consider using Tabasco sauce. It has only 26 mg of sodium per 5-7 drops.

FISH & SEAFOOD MAINS

Want to serve up a delicious seafood dish without fuss or mess? The saute function makes the Instant Pot® perfect for cooking— and never overcooking—seafood.

RED CLAM SAUCE

This recipe tastes like it's taken all day to prepare. What a great way to jazz up pasta sauce!
—JoAnn Brown, Latrobe, PA

Prep: 20 min.
Cook: 5 min. + releasing
Makes: 4 servings

- 1 **Tbsp. canola oil**
- 1 **medium onion, chopped**
- 2 **garlic cloves, minced**
- 2 **cans (6½ oz. each) chopped clams, undrained**
- 1 **can (14½ oz.) diced tomatoes, undrained**
- 1 **can (6 oz.) tomato paste**
- ¼ **cup minced fresh parsley**
- 1 **bay leaf**
- 1 **tsp. sugar**
- 1 **tsp. dried basil**
- ½ **tsp. dried thyme**
- 6 **oz. hot cooked linguine, drained**

1. Select saute setting on a 6-qt. electric pressure cooker and adjust for high heat. Add oil. When hot, add onion; saute until tender. Add garlic; cook 1 minute longer.

2. Stir in next eight ingredients. Lock lid; make sure vent is closed. Select manual setting; adjust pressure to high and set time for 3 minutes. When finished cooking, allow pressure to naturally release for 5 minutes, then quick-release any remaining pressure according to manufacturer's directions. Discard bay leaf. Serve with linguine.

1 SERVING: 217 cal., 5g fat (0 sat. fat), 33mg chol., 665mg sod., 32g carb. (10g sugars, 4g fiber), 14g pro. **DIABETIC EXCHANGES:** 2 starch, 2 lean meat, ½ fat.

WHY YOU'LL LOVE IT...

"I have made this receipe numerous times. It is absolutely wonderful and very easy to make. Even picky teens like it!"
—HARDSCRABBLEGIRL, TASTEOFHOME.COM

RISOTTO WITH SHRIMP & ASPARAGUS

This speedy method of cooking risotto works every time!
—Kim Gray, Davie, FL

Takes: 30 min
Makes: 8 servings

 3 Tbsp. unsalted butter
 1 small onion, finely diced
 6 garlic cloves, minced
 1⅔ cups uncooked arborio rice
 1 cup white wine
 4 cups reduced-sodium chicken broth
 ½ cup shredded Parmesan cheese, divided
 2 Tbsp. olive oil
 3 garlic cloves, minced
 2 lbs. uncooked shrimp (26-30 per lb.), peeled and deveined
 1 Tbsp. unsalted butter
 ½ cup Italian salad dressing
 1 lb. fresh asparagus, trimmed
 Salt and pepper to taste

1. Select saute setting on a 6-qt. electric pressure cooker and adjust for high heat; warm butter until melted. Add onion; cook 4-5 minutes. Add garlic; cook 1 minute. Add rice; cook and stir 2 minutes. Stir in ½ cup wine; cook and stir until absorbed. Add remaining wine, broth and ¼ cup cheese. Lock lid; make sure vent is closed. Select manual setting; adjust pressure to high. Set the time for 8 minutes. When finished cooking, quick-release pressure according to manufacturer's directions; stir.

2. Meanwhile, heat oil in a large skillet over medium-high heat. Add garlic; cook 1 minute. Add shrimp; cook and stir until the shrimp begin to turn pink, about 5 minutes. Add butter and dressing; stir until butter melts. Reduce heat. Add asparagus; cook until tender, 3-5 minutes. Serve over risotto. Season with salt and pepper. Sprinkle with the remaining cheese.

1 SERVING: 424 cal., 15g fat (6g sat. fat), 157mg chol., 661mg sod., 39g carb. (3g sugars, 1g fiber), 26g pro.

TEST KITCHEN TIP
To make risotto on the stovetop, bring broth to a simmer; keep hot. In a saucepan, heat 3 Tbsp. butter over medium-high heat. Add onion; cook 3 minutes. Add garlic and rice; cook and stir 2 minutes. Stir in wine; cook until the wine is absorbed. Stir in 1 cup hot broth. Reduce heat to maintain a simmer; cook and stir until the broth is absorbed. Add the remaining broth, ½ cup at a time, stirring until broth has been absorbed after each addition, until rice is tender. Prepare shrimp and asparagus as directed above.

ITALIAN SHRIMP & PASTA

This dish will remind you a bit of classic shrimp Creole, but it has a surprise Italian twist. Pressure cooking gives it hands-off ease—perfect for company.
—Karen Edwards, Sanford, ME

Prep: 20 min.
Cook: 20 min.
Makes: 6 servings

2 Tbsp. canola oil
4 boneless skinless
   chicken thighs (about
   1 lb.), cut into 2x1-in.
   strips
1 can (28 oz.) crushed
   tomatoes
1½ cups water
2 celery ribs, chopped
1 medium green pepper,
   cut into 1-in. pieces
1 medium onion, coarsely
   chopped
2 garlic cloves, minced
1 Tbsp. sugar
½ tsp. salt
½ tsp. Italian seasoning
⅛ to ¼ tsp. cayenne
   pepper
1 bay leaf
1 cup uncooked orzo or
   other small pasta
1 lb. peeled and deveined
   cooked shrimp
   (31-40 per lb.)

1. Select saute setting on a 6-qt. electric pressure cooker and adjust for high heat. Add 1 Tbsp. oil. When hot, brown the chicken in batches, adding oil as needed. Stir in the next 11 ingredients. Lock lid; make sure vent is closed. Select manual setting; adjust pressure to high and set time for 8 minutes. When finished cooking, quick-release any remaining pressure according to manufacturer's directions.

2. Discard bay leaf. Select saute setting and adjust for high heat. Stir in orzo. Cook until al dente, stirring often. Stir in shrimp; cook until the shrimp are heated through, about 2 minutes more.

1 SERVING: 418 cal., 12g fat (2g sat. fat), 165mg chol., 611mg sod., 40g carb. (10g sugars, 4g fiber), 36g pro.

TEST KITCHEN TIP
Orzo is rice-shaped pasta. You can find it in the pasta aisle of your grocery store.

CAROLINA SHRIMP & CHEDDAR GRITS

Shrimp and grits are a house favorite—if only we could agree on a recipe! I stirred things up with cheddar and Cajun seasoning to find a winner.
—Charlotte Price, Raleigh, NC

Prep: 15 min.
Cook: 20 min. + releasing
Makes: 6 servings

- 4 **cups water**
- 1 **large garlic cloves, minced**
- ½ **tsp. salt**
- ¼ **tsp. pepper**
- 1 **cup uncooked stone-ground grits**
- 2 **cups shredded cheddar cheese**
- ¼ **cup butter, cubed**
- 1 **lb. peeled and deveined cooked shrimp (31-40 per lb.)**
- 2 **medium tomatoes, seeded and finely chopped**
- 4 **green onions, finely chopped**
- 2 **Tbsp. minced fresh parsley**
- 4 **tsp. lemon juice**
- 2 **to 3 tsp. Cajun seasoning**

Select saute setting on a 6-qt. electric pressure cooker and adjust for high heat. Add the first four ingredients and stir to combine; bring to a boil. Slowly add the grits, stirring constantly to avoid lumps. Select saute setting, reduce heat to low and cook about 15 minutes, stirring occasionally. Stir in cheese and butter until melted. Stir in the remaining ingredients. Cook for 3-4 minutes or until heated through.

1 SERVING: 417 cal., 22g fat (13g sat. fat), 175mg chol., 788mg sod., 27g carb. (2g sugars, 2g fiber), 27g pro.

WHY YOU'LL LOVE IT...

"The first time I had shrimp and grits was a couple of years ago at a restaurant. It was just about the best thing I had ever eaten. Made this recipe today and it is fantastic! Serving with green onions and Tabasco at the table made it even better. Thanks for sharing!"
—MLGRAHAM, TASTEOFHOME.COM

TUNA NOODLE CASSEROLE

We tweaked this family-friendly classic to work for the pressure cooker. What a great meal-in-one dish. It's easy, wholesome and totally homemade!
—*Taste of Home* Test Kitchen

Prep: 25 min.
Cook: 15 min. + releasing
Makes: 10 servings

- ¼ cup butter, cubed
- ½ lb. sliced fresh mushrooms
- 1 medium onion, chopped
- 1 medium sweet pepper, chopped
- 1 tsp. salt, divided
- 1 tsp. pepper, divided
- 2 garlic cloves, minced
- ¼ cup all-purpose flour
- 2 cups reduced-sodium chicken broth
- 2 cups half-and-half cream
- 4 cups (8 oz.) uncooked egg noodles
- 3 cans (5 oz. each) light tuna in water
- 2 Tbsp. lemon juice
- 2 cups shredded Monterey Jack cheese
- 2 cups frozen peas, thawed
- 2 cups crushed potato chips

1. Select saute setting on a 6-qt. electric pressure cooker and adjust for high heat. Add butter. When melted, add mushrooms, onion, sweet pepper, ½ tsp. salt and ½ tsp. pepper; cook and stir until vegetables are tender, 6-8 minutes. Add garlic; cook 1 minute longer. Stir in flour until blended. Gradually whisk in broth. Bring to a boil, stirring constantly; cook and stir until thickened, 1-2 minutes. Stir in cream and noodles. Lock lid; make sure vent is closed. Select manual setting; adjust pressure to high and set time for 3 minutes. When finished cooking, allow pressure to naturally release for 3 minutes, then quick-release any remaining pressure according to manufacturer's directions.

2. Meanwhile, in a small bowl, combine tuna, lemon juice and the remaining salt and pepper. Select saute setting and adjust for low heat. Stir cheese, tuna mixture and peas into noodle mixture. Cook until heated through. Just before serving, sprinkle with potato chips.

1 SERVING: 393 cal., 21g fat (12g sat. fat), 84mg chol., 752mg sod., 28g carb. (5g sugars, 3g fiber), 22g pro.

TEST KITCHEN TIP

Canned mushrooms also work in this recipe. You can use frozen mixed peas and carrots for more veggie variety.

BUFFALO SHRIMP MAC & CHEESE

For a rich, creamy and slightly spicy shrimp and pasta recipe, you can't beat this crowd-pleasing dish. It's a nice new twist on popular Buffalo chicken dishes.
—Robin Haas, Cranston, RI

Prep: 15 min.
Cook: 10 min. + releasing
Makes: 6 servings

- 2 cups 2% milk
- 1 cup half-and-half cream
- 1 Tbsp. unsalted butter
- 1 tsp. ground mustard
- ½ tsp. onion powder
- ¼ tsp. white pepper
- ¼ tsp. ground nutmeg
- 1½ cups uncooked elbow macaroni
- 2 cups shredded cheddar cheese
- 1 cup shredded Gouda or Swiss cheese
- ¾ lb. frozen cooked salad shrimp, thawed
- 1 cup crumbled blue cheese
- 2 Tbsp. Louisiana-style hot sauce
- 2 Tbsp. minced fresh chives
- 2 Tbsp. minced fresh parsley
  Additional Louisiana-style hot sauce, optional

1. In a 6-qt. electric pressure cooker, combine the first seven ingredients; stir in macaroni. Lock lid; make sure vent is closed. Select manual setting; adjust pressure to high and set time for 3 minutes. When finished cooking, allow pressure to naturally release for 4 minutes, then quick-release any remaining pressure according to manufacturer's directions.

2. Select saute setting and adjust for normal heat. Stir in shredded cheeses, shrimp, blue cheese and hot sauce. Cook until heated through, 5 to 6 minutes. Just before serving, stir in chives, parsley and, if desired, additional hot sauce.

1 SERVING: 551 cal., 34g fat (20g sat. fat), 228mg chol., 1269mg sod., 22g carb. (7g sugars, 1g fiber), 38g pro.

TEST KITCHEN TIP
Make a Buffalo chicken version by adding cooked rotisserie chicken in place of the shrimp. Remember that crumbling your own blue cheese instead of buying prepackaged crumbles will make most any dish creamier.

PORK DINNERS

Mix up your dinner routine with these succulent pork entrees. Versatile, quick and loaded with flavor, they add flair to any meal plan.

PORK CHILI VERDE

Pork stews with jalapenos, onion, green enchilada sauce and spices in this flavor-packed Mexican dish. It's great on its own or stuffed in a warm tortilla with sour cream, grated cheese and olives on the side.
—Kimberly Burke, Chico, CA

Prep: 25 min.
Cook: 30 min + releasing
Makes: 8 servings

- 3 **Tbsp. canola oil**
- 1 **(3 lbs.) boneless pork sirloin roast, cut into 1-in. cubes**
- 4 **medium carrot, sliced**
- 1 **medium onion, thinly sliced**
- 4 **garlic cloves, minced**
- 1 **can (28 oz.) green enchilada sauce**
- ¼ **cup cold water**
- 2 **jalapeno pepper, seeded and chopped**
- 1 **cup minced fresh cilantro**
  Hot cooked rice
  Flour tortillas (8 in.)

1. Select saute setting on a 6-qt. electric pressure cooker and adjust for high heat; add oil. In batches, saute the pork, carrots, onion and garlic until browned. Return all items to the pressure cooker.

2. Add enchilada sauce, water, jalapenos and cilantro. Lock lid; make sure vent is closed. Select manual; adjust pressure to high and set time for 30 minutes. When finished cooking, allow pressure to naturally release for 10 minutes and then quick-release any remaining pressure according to the manufacturer's instructions. Serve with rice and tortillas.

1 SERVING: 312 cal., 12g fat (4g sat. fat), 102mg chol., 616mg sod., 11g carb. (5g sugars, 1g fiber), 37g pro.

DID YOU KNOW?
Pork sirloin roast is one end of a pork loin roast; you can use pork loin for this recipe as well. Pork tenderloin is a separate cut, and lends itself to quick cooking and roasting; it's not a good substitution here.

MESQUITE RIBS

When we're missing the grill during winter, these tangy ribs give us that same smoky barbecue taste we love. They're so simple, and fall-off-the-bone delicious, too!
—Sue Evans, Marquette, MI

Prep: 10 min. + broiling
Cook: 35 min. + releasing
Makes: 8 servings

- 1 **cup water**
- 2 **Tbsp. cider vinegar**
- 1 **Tbsp. soy sauce**
- 4 **lbs. pork baby back ribs, cut into serving-size portions**
- 2 **Tbsp. mesquite seasoning**
- ¾ **cup barbecue sauce, divided**

1. Combine water, vinegar and soy sauce in a 6-qt. electric pressure cooker. Rub ribs with mesquite seasoning; add to pressure cooker. Lock lid in place; make sure vent is closed. Select manual setting; adjust pressure to high, and set time to 35 minutes. When finished cooking, naturally release pressure for 10 minutes, then quick-release any remaining pressure according to manufacturer's directions.

2. Remove ribs to a foil-lined baking sheet. Preheat broiler. Brush ribs with barbecue sauce. Broil 4-6 in. from heat until glazed. Serve with additional barbecue sauce if desired.

1 SERVING: 329 cal., 21g fat (8g sat. fat), 81mg chol., 678mg sod., 10g carb. (8g sugars, 0 fiber), 23g pro.

SWEET & SOUR PORK

Even though a co-worker gave me this recipe more than 20 years ago, my family still enjoys it today. It's a lovely meal-in-one dish.
—Martha Nickerson, Hancock, ME

Prep: 20 min.
Cook: 15 min.
Makes: 6 servings

- 2 Tbsp. plus 1½ tsp. paprika
- 1½ lbs. boneless pork loin roast, cut into 1-in. strips
- 1 Tbsp. canola oil
- 1 can (20 oz.) unsweetened pineapple chunks
- 1 medium onion, chopped
- 1 medium green pepper, chopped
- ¼ cup cider vinegar
- 3 Tbsp. packed brown sugar
- 3 Tbsp. reduced-sodium soy sauce
- 1 Tbsp. Worcestershire sauce
- ½ tsp. salt
- 2 Tbsp. cornstarch
- ¼ cup cold water
  Thinly sliced/chopped green onions, optional
  Hot cooked rice, optional

1. Place paprika in a large resealable plastic bag. Add pork, a few pieces at a time, and shake to coat. Select saute setting on a 6-qt. electric pressure cooker and adjust for medium heat; add oil. Brown the pork in batches, then return all pork to pressure cooker.

2. Drain pineapple, reserving juice; refrigerate the pineapple. Add the pineapple juice, onion, green pepper, vinegar, brown sugar, soy sauce, Worcestershire sauce and salt to the pressure cooker. Lock lid; make sure vent is closed. Select manual; adjust pressure to high and set time for 10 minutes. When finished cooking, quick-release pressure according to the manufacturer's instructions.

3. Select saute setting and adjust for high heat; bring liquid to a boil. In a small bowl, mix cornstarch and water until smooth; gradually stir into pork mixture. Add pineapple. Cook and stir until sauce is thickened, 1-2 minutes. If desired, sprinkle with green onions and serve over rice.

1 SERVING: 312 cal., 10g fat (3g sat. fat), 73mg chol., 592mg sod., 28g carb. (21g sugars, 2g fiber), 27g pro.

CARNE GUISADA

When we were living in another state for a while, my boyfriend and I grew homesick for the spicy flavors back in Texas. We've made this recipe a few times now. It goes really well with homemade flour tortillas. We love it over rice, too.
—Kelly Evans, Denton, TX

Prep: 25 min.
Cook: 50 min. + releasing
Makes: 12 servings
    (about 2 qt.)

- 1 bottle (12 oz.) beer
- 2 Tbsp. tomato paste
- 1 jalapeno pepper, seeded and chopped
- 4 tsp. Worcestershire sauce
- 1 bay leaf
- 2 to 3 tsp. crushed red pepper flakes
- 2 tsp. chili powder
- 1½ tsp. ground cumin
- ½ tsp. salt
- ½ tsp. paprika
- 2 garlic cloves, minced
- ½ tsp. red wine vinegar
    Dash liquid smoke, optional
- 1 boneless pork shoulder butt roast (3 lbs.), cut into 2-in. pieces
- 1 medium onion, chopped
- 2 large red potatoes, unpeeled and chopped
- ¼ cup all-purpose flour
- ¼ cup water
    Whole wheat tortillas, cooked brown rice, lime wedges and minced fresh cilantro, optional

1. In a 6-qt. electric pressure cooker, mix first 12 ingredients and, if desired, liquid smoke. Stir in pork and onion. Lock lid; make sure the vent is closed. Select manual setting; adjust pressure to high and set time for 45 minutes. Quick-release the pressure; add potatoes. Lock lid in place and cook an additional 5 minutes. When finished cooking, allow pressure to naturally release for 10 minutes and then quick-release any remaining pressure according to manufacturer's instructions.

2. Discard bay leaf; skim fat from cooking juices. Select saute setting and adjust for normal heat; bring a to boil. Combine flour and ¼ cup water; stir into simmering sauce. Cook until thickened and boiling, 1-2 minutes Shred pork slightly with two forks; toss with sauce. Serve with remaining ingredients as desired.

1 SERVING: 261 cal., 12g fat (4g sat. fat), 67mg chol., 200mg sod., 16g carb. (3g sugars, 2g fiber), 21g pro.

WHY YOU'LL LOVE IT...

"Made my house smell terrific and tasted even better! The leftovers were great in quesadillas!"
—ANGIEACT1, TASTEOFHOME.COM

SICILIAN MEAT SAUCE

People have told me this is better than the gravy their Sicilian grandmothers used to make. But don't tell the older generation that!
—Emory Doty, Jasper, GA

Prep: 30 min.
Cook: 40 min. + releasing
Makes: 12 servings

- 3 Tbsp. olive oil, divided
- 2 lbs. boneless country-style pork ribs
- 1 medium onion, chopped
- 3 to 5 garlic cloves, minced
- 2 cans (28 oz. each) crushed or diced tomatoes
- 1 can (6 oz.) Italian tomato paste
- 3 bay leaves
- 2 Tbsp. chopped fresh parsley
- 2 Tbsp. chopped capers, drained
- ½ tsp. dried basil
- ½ tsp. dried rosemary, crushed
- ½ tsp. dried thyme
- ½ tsp. crushed red pepper flakes
- ½ tsp. salt
- ½ tsp. sugar
- 1 cup beef broth
- ½ cup dry red wine or additional beef broth
  Hot cooked pasta
  Grated Parmesan cheese, optional

1. Select saute setting on a 6-qt. electric pressure cooker and adjust for high heat; add 2 Tbsp. olive oil. In batches, brown the pork on all sides. Set aside.

2. Add remaining oil to pressure cooker; saute onion for 2 minutes. Add garlic; cook 1 minute more. Add the next 11 ingredients. Transfer meat to pressure cooker. Pour in broth and red wine; bring to a light boil. Lock lid; make sure vent is closed. Select manual setting; adjust pressure to high and set time for 35 minutes. When finished cooking, allow pressure
to naturally release for 10 minutes and then quick-release any remaining pressure according to manufacturer's instructions.

3. Discard bay leaves. Remove meat from pressure cooker; shred or pull apart, discarding bones. Return meat to sauce. Serve over pasta; if desired, sprinkle with Parmesan cheese.

1 SERVING: 214 cal., 11g fat (3g sat. fat), 44mg chol., 822mg sod., 13g carb. (8g sugars, 3g fiber), 16g pro.

DID YOU KNOW?
Debate rages whether Italian-style tomato sauce is properly called "sauce" or "gravy," and is largely a regional preference in the U.S. "Ragu," however, is reserved for sauce (or gravy!) that contains meat.

MEXICAN CARNITAS

Carnitas are small pieces of crisp pork that are popular in Mexico. The secret to this recipe is the citrus and quick frying. Be sure to drain the meat well before you place it in the oil, though, or the oil will splatter and pop.
—Patricia Collins, Imbler, OR

Prep: 15 min.
Cook: 40 min. + releasing
Makes: 16 servings

1 **boneless pork shoulder roast (3 to 4 lbs.), cut into 2-in. cubes**
1 **tsp. salt**
1 **tsp. pepper**
6 **large garlic cloves, minced**
½ **cup fresh cilantro leaves, chopped**
3 **large navel oranges**
1 **large lemon**
 Canola oil or bacon drippings
16 **flour tortillas (8 in.), warmed**
 Optional toppings: chopped tomatoes, shredded cheddar cheese, sliced green onions, sour cream and sliced avocado

1. Place pork in a 6-qt. electric pressure cooker. Season with salt and pepper; sprinkle with garlic and cilantro. Squeeze juice from the oranges and lemon over the meat.

2. Lock lid; make sure vent is closed. Select manual setting; adjust pressure to high and set time for 25 minutes. When finished cooking, allow the pressure to naturally release for 10 minutes and then quick-release the remaining pressure according to the manufacturer's directions. With a slotted spoon, remove the meat and drain well on paper towels. Pour the cooking liquid into a glass measuring cup and let the fat rise to the surface. Skim fat from surface and place in the cooker insert; discard the remaining cooking liquid.

3. Select saute setting and adjust for high heat. Add enough canola oil or bacon drippings to measure ½-in. depth. When oil is hot, add the pork in batches and fry until dark golden brown and crisp. Remove and keep warm. Repeat with remaining pork.

4. Serve warm in tortillas with toppings of your choice.

FREEZE OPTION: Freeze cooled pork mixture in freezer containers. To use, partially thaw in refrigerator overnight. Fry meat in batches as directed until crisp and brown. Serve as directed.

1 SERVING: 391 cal., 20g fat (5g sat. fat), 51mg chol., 435mg sod., 32g carb. (3g sugars, 3g fiber), 19g pro.

CHAR SIU PORK

The Asian influence on food here in Hawaii inspired this juicy pork. It's tasty as is, in a bun or over rice. Use any leftovers with fried rice, ramen and salads.
—Karen Naihe, Kamuela, HI

Prep: 25 min. + marinating
Cook: 1¼ hours + releasing
Makes: 8 servings

- ½ **cup honey**
- ½ **cup hoisin sauce**
- ¼ **cup soy sauce**
- ¼ **cup ketchup**
- 4 **garlic cloves, minced**
- 4 **tsp. minced fresh gingerroot**
- 1 **tsp. Chinese five-spice powder**
- 1 **boneless pork shoulder butt roast (3 to 4 lbs.)**
- ½ **cup chicken broth**
  Fresh cilantro leaves

1. Combine the first seven ingredients; pour into a large resealable plastic bag. Cut roast in half; add to bag and turn to coat. Refrigerate overnight.

2. Transfer pork and marinade to a 6-qt. electric pressure cooker. Add chicken broth. Lock lid; make sure vent is closed. Select manual setting; adjust pressure to high and set time for 75 minutes. When finished cooking, allow pressure to naturally release for 10 minutes, then quick-release any remaining pressure according to manufacturer's directions.

3. Remove pork; when cool enough to handle, shred meat using two forks. Skim fat from cooking juices. Return pork to the pressure cooker. Select saute setting and adjust for normal heat; heat through. Top with fresh cilantro.

4 OZ. COOKED PORK: 392 cal., 18g fat (6g sat. fat), 102mg chol., 981mg sod., 27g carb. (24g sugars, 1g fiber), 31g pro.

TEST KITCHEN TIP
You can freeze large pieces of unpeeled gingerroot in a freezer-storage bag. When you need some, simply grate the frozen ginger and pop it back in the freezer. No more shriveled ginger in the bottom of your produce drawer.

EASY RIGATONI WITH SAUSAGE & PEAS

With a tomato-y meat sauce and tangy goat cheese, this weeknight wonder is my version of comfort food. You just want to have bowl after bowl!
—Lizzie Munro, Brooklyn, NY

Takes: 30 min.
Makes: 6 servings

- 1 **lb. bulk Italian sausage**
- 4 **garlic cloves, minced**
- ¼ **cup tomato paste**
- 12 **oz. uncooked rigatoni or large tube pasta**
- 1½ **cups frozen peas**
- 1 **can (28 oz.) crushed tomatoes**
- ½ **tsp. dried basil**
- ¼ **to ½ tsp. crushed red pepper flakes**
- 4 **cups water**
- ½ **cup heavy whipping cream**
- ½ **cup crumbled goat or feta cheese**
     Thinly sliced fresh basil, optional

1. Select saute setting on a 6-qt. electric pressure cooker and adjust for high heat. Cook and crumble sausage until no longer pink, 4-6 minutes. Add garlic; cook 1 minute longer. Add tomato paste; cook and stir until the meat is coated, 1-2 minutes. Stir in next five ingredients; pour in water. Lock lid; make sure vent is closed. Select manual setting; adjust pressure to low and set time for 6 minutes. When finished cooking, quick-release pressure according to manufacturer's directions.

2. Stir in cream; heat through. Top with cheese and, if desired, fresh basil.

1⅔ CUPS: 563 cal., 28g fat (12g sat. fat), 75mg chol., 802mg sod., 60g carb. (11g sugars, 7g fiber), 23g pro.

CRANBERRY-MUSTARD PORK LOIN

This dressed-up pork loin is so simple to make that you only have to spend a few minutes preparing it. It's a family favorite because it is so tasty, and a favorite of mine because it's so fast and easy!
—Laura Cook, Wildwood, MO

Prep: 15 min.
Cook: 30 min. + releasing
Makes: 8 servings

- 1 **boneless pork loin roast (2 lbs.)**
- 1 **can (14 oz.) whole-berry cranberry sauce**
- ¼ **cup Dijon mustard**
- 3 **Tbsp. packed brown sugar**
- 3 **Tbsp. lemon juice**
- 1 **Tbsp. cornstarch**
- ¼ **cup cold water**

1. Place roast in a 6-qt. electric pressure cooker. Combine the cranberry sauce, mustard, brown sugar and lemon juice; pour over roast. Lock lid; make sure vent is closed. Select manual setting; adjust pressure to high and set time for 25 minutes. When finished cooking, allow pressure to naturally release for 10 minutes and then quick-release any remaining pressure according to the manufacturer's instructions. Remove roast and keep warm.

2. Strain cooking juices into a 2-cup measuring cup; add enough water to measure 2 cups. Return juices to the pressure cooker. Select saute setting and adjust for high heat; bring liquid to a boil. In a small bowl, mix cornstarch and water until smooth; gradually stir into cooking juices. Cook and stir until sauce is thickened, 1-2 minutes. Serve with pork.

1 SERVING: 255 cal., 6g fat (2g sat. fat), 56mg chol., 236mg sod., 28g carb. (19g sugars, 1g fiber), 22g pro.

WHY YOU'LL LOVE IT...

"I made this for dinner tonight and it was a huge hit! My kids kept asking for more! Very good flavor and super easy."
—WADDINGTON6,
TASTEOFHOME.COM

MEMPHIS-STYLE RIBS

After my dad and I had dinner at Tennessee's legendary Rendezvous restaurant, I was inspired to create my own version of tasty dry-rub Memphis ribs. Smoked paprika in the rub mimics the flavor the ribs would get from grilling over hot coals.
—Matthew Hass, Franklin, WI

Prep: 15 min.
Cook: 20 min+ releasing
Makes: 6 servings

- ½ **cup white vinegar**
- ½ **cup water**
- 3 **Tbsp. smoked paprika**
- 2 **Tbsp. brown sugar**
- 2 **tsp. salt**
- 2 **tsp. coarsely ground pepper**
- 1 **tsp. garlic powder**
- 1 **tsp. onion powder**
- 1 **tsp. ground cumin**
- 1 **tsp. ground mustard**
- 1 **tsp. dried thyme**
- 1 **tsp. dried oregano**
- 1 **tsp. celery salt**
- ¾ **tsp. cayenne pepper**
- 2 **racks pork baby back ribs (about 5 lbs.)**

1. Combine vinegar and water; brush over ribs. Pour the remaining vinegar mixture into a 6-qt. electric pressure cooker. Mix together next 12 ingredients, reserving half. Sprinkle ribs with half of the seasoning blend. Cut ribs into serving-size pieces; transfer to pressure cooker.

2. Lock lid; make sure vent is closed. Select manual setting; adjust pressure to high and set time for 20 minutes. When finished cooking, allow pressure to naturally release for 10 minutes and then quick-release any remaining pressure according to the manufacturer's instructions. Remove ribs; skim fat from cooking juices. Using a clean brush, brush ribs generously with the skimmed cooking juices; sprinkle with the reserved seasoning. Serve ribs with the remaining juices.

1 SERVING: 509 cal., 35g fat (13g sat. fat), 136mg chol., 1137mg sod., 8g carb. (5g sugars, 2g fiber), 38g pro.

CAJUN PORK & RICE

I created this recipe after I returned home from traveling and had little food in the house. I used ingredients already available in the refrigerator and pantry. My husband loves this pork dish because it's tasty; I love it because it's easy!
—Allison Gapinski, Cary, NC

Prep: 20 min.
Cook: 20 min. + releasing
Makes: 4 servings

- 1 tsp. olive oil
- 1 medium green pepper, julienned
- 1½ tsp. ground cumin
- 1½ tsp. chili powder
- 1½ lbs. boneless pork loin chops
- 1 can (14½ oz.) petite diced tomatoes, undrained
- 1 small onion, finely chopped
- 1 celery rib, chopped
- 1 small carrot, julienned
- 1 garlic cloves, minced
- ½ tsp. Louisiana-style hot sauce
- ¼ tsp. salt
- ¾ cup reduced-sodium chicken broth
- 1½ cups uncooked instant rice

1. Select saute setting on a 6-qt. electric pressure cooker and adjust for high heat; add oil. Add green pepper; cook and stir 4-5 minutes or until crisp-tender. Remove and set aside. Select cancel setting to turn off saute function.

2. Mix cumin and chili powder; sprinkle pork chops with 2 tsp. spice mixture. Add pork to pressure cooker. In a small bowl, mix tomatoes, onion, celery, carrot, garlic, hot sauce, salt and remaining spice mixture; pour over pork. Lock lid; make sure vent is closed. Select manual setting; adjust pressure to high and set time for 6 minutes. When finished cooking, allow pressure to naturally release for 5 minutes and then quick-release any remaining pressure according to manufacturer's instructions.

3. Stir in chicken broth, breaking up pork into pieces. Select saute setting and adjust for normal heat; bring a to boil. Add rice. Cook 5 minutes longer or until rice is tender. Serve peppers with pork mixture.

1 SERVING: 423 cal., 12g fat (4g sat. fat), 82mg chol., 573mg sod., 40g carb. (6g sugars, 4g fiber), 38g pro. **DIABETIC EXCHANGES:** 5 lean meat, 2 starch, 1 vegetable.

CHINESE-STYLE RIBS

Soy, ginger, garlic and a dash of heat make these ribs a delight. That they can be on the table in under an hour, start to finish, makes them perfect for any weeknight dinner.
—Paula Marchesi, Lenhartsville, PA

Prep: 20 min.
Cook: 30 min. + releasing
Makes: 6 servings

- 3 lbs. boneless country-style pork ribs
- 6 green onions, cut into 1-in. pieces
- 1 can (8 oz.) sliced water chestnuts, drained
- ¾ cup hoisin sauce
- ½ cup water
- 3 Tbsp. soy sauce
- 2 Tbsp. sherry or chicken stock
- 5 garlic cloves, minced
- 1 Tbsp. minced fresh gingerroot
- 1 Tbsp. light corn syrup
- 1 Tbsp. orange marmalade
- 1 tsp. pumpkin pie spice
- ½ tsp. crushed red pepper flakes
- 1 to 2 Tbsp. cornstarch
- 2 Tbsp. water
  Hot cooked rice
  Thinly sliced / chopped green onions, optional

1. Place pork, green onions and water chestnuts in a 6-qt. electric pressure cooker. Mix hoisin sauce, water, soy sauce, sherry, garlic, gingerroot, corn syrup, marmalade, pie spice and pepper flakes in a bowl. Pour over pork. Lock lid; make sure vent is closed. Select manual setting; adjust pressure to high and set time for 25 minutes. When finished cooking, allow pressure to naturally release for 10 minutes and then quick-release any remaining pressure according to manufacturer's instructions.

2. Remove pork to a serving platter; keep warm. Skim the fat from the cooking juices. Select saute setting and adjust for normal heat. In a small bowl, mix cornstarch and water until smooth. Gradually stir cornstarch mixture into the pressure cooker. Bring to a boil; cook and stir until thickened, about 2 minutes. Serve with ribs, rice and, if desired, additional green onions.

1 SERVING: 493 cal., 22g fat (8g sat. fat), 132mg chol., 1115mg sod., 28g carb. (15g sugars, 2g fiber), 42g pro.

DID YOU KNOW?
Hoisin sauce is a thick spicy-sweet sauce used as a glaze or as a finishing touch for stir-fries. It's widely available in stores now. If you can't find it, you can make your own using soy sauce, peanut butter, molasses or honey, rice vinegar, minced garlic, sesame seed oil, Chinese hot sauce and black pepper.

POULTRY FAVORITES

When it comes to fast mealtime favorites, chicken and turkey are at the top of everyone's list. That's why these family cooks are happy to share their top picks for dinner success.

APPLE BALSAMIC CHICKEN

I just love the sweet-tart flavor balsamic vinegar gives to this easy dish. After just a few minutes in the pressure cooker, the chicken thighs are tender and flavorful.
—Juli Snaer, Enid, OK

Prep: 15 min.
Cook: 15 min. + releasing
Makes: 4 servings

- ½ cup chicken broth
- ¼ cup apple cider or juice
- ¼ cup balsamic vinegar
- 2 Tbsp. lemon juice
- ½ tsp. salt
- ½ tsp. garlic powder
- ½ tsp. dried thyme
- ½ tsp. paprika
- ½ tsp. pepper
- 4 bone-in chicken thighs (about 1½ lbs.), skin removed
- 2 Tbsp. butter
- 2 Tbsp. all-purpose flour

1. In a small bowl, combine the first nine ingredients. Place chicken in a 6-qt. electric pressure cooker; pour broth mixture over meat. Lock lid; make sure vent is closed. Select manual setting; adjust pressure to high and set time for 10 minutes. When finished cooking, allow pressure to naturally release for 10 minutes, then quick-release any remaining pressure according to manufacturer's directions.

2. Remove chicken; keep warm. Skim fat from cooking liquid. In a small saucepan, melt butter; whisk in flour until smooth. Gradually add cooking liquid. Cook and stir until sauce is thickened, 2-3 minutes. Serve with chicken.

1 SERVING: 277 cal., 15g fat (6g sat. fat), 103mg chol., 536mg sod., 9g carb. (4g sugars, 0 fiber), 25g pro.

DID YOU KNOW
Balsamic vinegar, which is produced in Italy, is aged in wooden barrels.

HULI HULI CHICKEN THIGHS

I'm allergic to most store-bought barbecue sauces, so when I found a marinade recipe I could use, I tweaked it a little and began using it with chicken thighs. My fiance loves this over Parmesan couscous.
—Erin Rockwell, Lowell, MA

Prep: 5 min.
Cook: 10 min. + releasing
Makes: 8 servings

- 1 cup crushed pineapple, drained
- ¾ cup ketchup
- ⅓ cup reduced-sodium soy sauce
- 3 Tbsp. packed brown sugar
- 3 Tbsp. lime juice
- 1 garlic clove, minced
- 8 boneless skinless chicken thighs (about 2 lbs.)
  Hot cooked rice
  Green onions, thinly sliced, optional

Mix first six ingredients. Place chicken in a 6-qt. electric pressure cooker; top with pineapple mixture. Lock lid; make sure vent is closed. Select manual setting; adjust pressure to high and set time for 10 minutes. When finished cooking, allow pressure to naturally release for 5 minutes and then quick-release any remaining pressure according to manufacturer's instructions. Serve with rice. If desired, top with green onions.

1 SERVING: 239 cal., 8g fat (2g sat. fat), 76mg chol., 733mg sod., 19g carb. (16g sugars, 0 fiber), 22g pro.

TURKEY WITH BERRY COMPOTE

This delicious dish is a great way to get the yummy turkey flavor my family craves without heating up the house. Best of all, the berries make the perfect summer sauce.
—Margaret Bracher, Robertsdale, AL

Prep: 15 min. + standing
Cook: 45 min. + releasing
Makes: 12 servings (3¼ cups compote)

- 1 **tsp. salt**
- ½ **tsp. garlic powder**
- ½ **tsp. dried thyme**
- ½ **tsp. pepper**
- 2 **boneless skinless turkey breast halves (2 lbs. each)**
- ⅓ **cup water**

COMPOTE

- 2 **medium apples, peeled and finely chopped**
- 2 **cups fresh raspberries**
- 2 **cups fresh blueberries**
- 1 **cup white grape juice**
- ¼ **tsp. crushed red pepper flakes**
- ¼ **tsp. ground ginger**

1. Mix salt, garlic powder, thyme and pepper; rub over turkey breasts. Place in a 6-qt. electric pressure cooker. Pour water around turkey. Lock lid; make sure vent is closed. Select manual setting; adjust pressure to high and set time for 30 minutes. When finished cooking, allow pressure to naturally release for 10 minutes, then quick-release any remaining pressure according to manufacturer's directions. A thermometer inserted in turkey breasts should read at least 165°.

2. Carefully remove turkey and cooking juices from pressure cooker; tent with foil. Let stand before slicing while you prepare the compote.

3. In pressure cooker, select saute setting, and adjust for high heat. Add compote ingredients. Bring to a boil. Reduce the heat to medium; cook, uncovered, stirring occasionally, until slightly thickened and apples are tender, 15-20 minutes. Serve turkey with compote.

1 SERVING: 215 cal., 1g fat (0 sat. fat), 94mg chol., 272mg sod., 12g carb. (8g sugars, 2g fiber), 38g pro.

MINI TERIYAKI TURKEY SANDWICHES

Preparing pulled turkey in a delicious teriyaki sauce for these snack-size sandwiches is a breeze using a pressure cooker. Serving them on lightly toasted sweet dinner rolls is an ideal finishing touch.
—Amanda Hoop, Seaman, OH

Prep: 20 min.
Cook: 30 min. + releasing
Makes: 20 servings

- 2 **boneless skinless turkey breast halves (2 lbs. each)**
- ⅔ **cup packed brown sugar**
- ⅔ **cup reduced-sodium soy sauce**
- ¼ **cup cider vinegar**
- 3 **garlic cloves, minced**
- 1 **Tbsp. minced fresh gingerroot**
- ½ **tsp. pepper**
- 2 **Tbsp. cornstarch**
- 2 **Tbsp. cold water**
- 20 **Hawaiian sweet rolls**
- 2 **Tbsp. butter, melted**

1. Place turkey in a 6-qt. electric pressure cooker. In a small bowl, combine next six ingredients; pour over turkey. Lock lid; make sure vent is closed. Select manual setting; adjust pressure to high and set time for 25 minutes. When finished cooking, allow pressure to naturally release for 10 minutes, then quick-release any remaining pressure according to manufacturer's directions.

2. Remove turkey from pressure cooker. Select saute setting and adjust for high heat; bring juices to a boil. In a small bowl, mix cornstarch and water until smooth; gradually stir into cooking juices. Bring to a boil; cook and stir for 2 minutes or until sauce is thickened. When cool enough to handle, shred meat with two forks; return meat to pressure cooker. Stir to heat through.

3. Preheat oven to 325°. Split rolls; brush cut sides with butter. Place on an ungreased baking sheet, cut side up. Bake until golden brown, 8-10 minutes. Spoon ⅓ cup turkey mixture on roll bottoms. Replace tops.

1 MINI SANDWICH: 252 cal., 5g fat (2g sat. fat), 70mg chol., 501mg sod., 25g carb. (13g sugars, 1g fiber), 26g pro.

TEST KITCHEN TIP
This recipe also works great with boneless, skinless chicken breasts. To spice things up, add a dash of crushed red pepper flakes or slices of fresh jalapeno.

BLACK BEAN CHICKEN NACHOS

One of my favorite local restaurants has the best chicken nachos. The dish inspired me to create my own—with the added convenience of using my all-in-one cooker. I recommend fresh cilantro because it makes the nachos pop with flavor.
—Natalie Hess, Cedar Rapids, IA

Prep: 10 min.
Cook: 8 min. + releasing
Makes: 8 servings

- 1½ lbs. boneless skinless chicken breasts
- 2 jars (16 oz. each) black bean and corn salsa
- 1 medium green pepper, chopped
- 1 medium sweet red pepper, chopped
- 1 pkg. (12 oz.) tortilla chips
- 2 cups shredded Mexican cheese blend
  Optional toppings: minced fresh cilantro, pickled jalapeno slices and sour cream

1. Place chicken, salsa and peppers in a 6-qt. electric pressure cooker. Lock lid; make sure vent is closed. Select manual setting; adjust pressure to high and set time for 8 minutes. When finished cooking, allow pressure to naturally release for 7 minutes and then quick-release any remaining pressure according to manufacturer's instructions.

2. Remove chicken; shred with two forks. Return to pressure cooker. Using a slotted spoon, serve chicken over chips; sprinkle with cheese and, if desired, cilantro. Serve with the toppings as desired.

1 SERVING: 280 cal., 11g fat (5g sat. fat), 72mg chol., 708mg sod., 20g carb. (5g sugars, 8g fiber), 27g pro.

TEST KITCHEN TIP
Use any leftover chicken mixture for fast tacos or burritos the next day.

BBQ CHICKEN & SMOKED SAUSAGE

My party-ready barbecue recipe works well for weeknight meals, too. With just a few minutes of prep time, you still get that low-and-slow flavor everybody loves. Throw in minced jalapenos for extra oomph.
—Kimberly Young, Mesquite, TX

Prep: 10 min.
Cook: 25 min.
Makes: 8 servings

- 1 **medium onion, chopped**
- 1 **large sweet red pepper, cut into 1-in. pieces**
- 4 **bone-in chicken thighs, skin removed**
- 4 **chicken drumsticks, skin removed**
- 1 **pkg. (12 oz.) smoked sausage links, cut into 1-in. pieces**
- 1 **cup chicken broth**
- 1 **cup barbecue sauce**
  Sliced seeded jalapeno pepper, optional

1. Place first six ingredients in a 6-qt. electric pressure cooker; top with barbecue sauce. Lock lid; make sure vent is closed. Select manual setting; adjust pressure to high, and set time for 12 minutes. When finished cooking, quick-release pressure according to manufacturer's directions (a thermometer inserted in chicken should read at least 170°). Remove chicken, sausage and vegetables from cooker; keep warm.

2. Select saute setting and adjust for high heat; bring liquid to a boil. Reduce heat; simmer until thickened, 12-15 minutes, stirring occasionally.

3. Serve chicken, sausage and vegetables with sauce. If desired, top with jalapeno.

1 SERVING: 338 cal., 18g fat (7g sat. fat), 93mg chol., 1009mg sod., 18g carb. (14g sugars, 1g fiber), 25g pro.

CHICKEN TIKKA MASALA

The flavors of this Indian-style entree keep me coming back for more. The dish isn't fancy, and it's simply spiced—but it's simply amazing.
—Jaclyn Bell, Logan, UT

Prep: 20 min.
Cook: 20 min.
Makes: 8 servings

2 Tbsp. olive oil
½ large onion, finely chopped
4½ tsp. minced fresh gingerroot
4 garlic cloves, minced
1 Tbsp. garam masala
2½ tsp. salt
1½ tsp. ground cumin
1 tsp. paprika
¾ tsp. pepper
½ tsp. cayenne pepper
¼ tsp. ground cinnamon
2½ lbs. boneless skinless chicken breasts, cut into 1½-in. cubes
1 can (29 oz.) tomato puree
⅓ cup water
1 jalapeno pepper, halved and seeded
1 bay leaf
1 Tbsp. cornstarch
1½ cups (12 oz.) plain yogurt
Hot cooked basmati rice
Chopped fresh cilantro, optional

1. Select saute setting on a 6-qt. electric pressure cooker and adjust for medium heat; add oil. Cook onion until tender. Add gingerroot and garlic; cook 1 minute. Stir in seasonings and cook 30 seconds. Add chicken, tomato puree, water, jalapeno and bay leaf.

2. Lock lid; make sure vent is closed. Select manual setting; adjust pressure to high and set time for 10 minutes. When finished cooking, quick-release the pressure according to manufacturer's directions. Discard bay leaf.

3. Select saute setting and adjust for medium heat; bring mixture to a boil. In a small bowl, mix cornstarch and yogurt until smooth; gradually stir into sauce. Cook and stir until sauce is thickened, about 3 minutes. Serve with rice. If desired, sprinkle with cilantro.

1 CUP CHICKEN MIXTURE: 279 cal., 8g fat (2g sat. fat), 84mg chol., 856mg sod., 13g carb. (5g sugars, 2g fiber), 32g pro. **DIABETIC EXCHANGES:** 4 lean meat, 1 starch, 1 fat.

DID YOU KNOW
Tikka masala has no standard recipe. It varies from family to family in Indian culture. Traditionally, chicken is marinated in the yogurt and spice mixture and cooked in a tandoori oven.

CHICKEN WITH OLIVES & ARTICHOKES

My grandmother came from the region around Seville, Spain, where olives and red wine are produced. It's no surprise that those ingredients get starring roles in her chicken dish.
—Suzette Zara, Scottsdale, AZ

Prep: 30 min.
Cook: 25 min. + releasing
Makes: 8 servings

- ¼ cup all-purpose flour
- ½ tsp. garlic salt
- ¼ tsp. pepper
- 8 bone-in chicken thighs (3 lbs.), skin removed if desired
- 1 Tbsp. olive oil
- 4 garlic cloves, thinly sliced
- 1 Tbsp. grated lemon peel
- 1 tsp. dried thyme
- ½ tsp. dried rosemary, crushed
- 1 can (14 oz.) water-packed quartered artichoke hearts, drained
- ½ cup pimiento-stuffed olives
- 1 bay leaf
- 1½ cups orange juice
- ¾ cup chicken broth
- 2 Tbsp. honey

GREMOLATA
- ¼ cup minced fresh basil
- 1 tsp. grated lemon peel
- 1 garlic clove, minced

1. In a shallow bowl, mix flour, garlic salt and pepper. Dip chicken thighs in flour mixture to coat both sides; shake off any excess.

2. Select saute setting on a 6-qt. electric pressure cooker and adjust for normal heat; add oil. In batches, brown the chicken on all sides.

3. Sprinkle garlic, lemon peel, thyme and rosemary over chicken. Top with artichoke hearts, olives and bay leaf. In a bowl, mix orange juice, broth and honey; pour over top. Lock lid; make sure vent is closed. Select manual setting; adjust pressure to high and set time for 15 minutes. When finished cooking, allow pressure to naturally release for 10 minutes and then quick-release any remaining pressure according to manufacturer's instructions. Remove bay leaf.

4. Mix gremolata ingredients in a small bowl. Sprinkle over chicken and artichoke mixture.

1 CHICKEN THIGH WITH 2 TBSP. ARTICHOKE MIXTURE AND 1½ TSP. GREMOLATA: 434 cal., 21g fat (4g sat. fat), 81mg chol., 971mg sod., 34g carb. (17g sugars, 1g fiber), 26g pro.

CHICKEN CACCIATORE

My husband and I own and operate a busy farm, and many days there's just no time for cooking. It's really nice to come into the house at night and have this hearty dinner ready in about half an hour.
—Aggie Arnold-Norman, Liberty, PA

Prep: 15 min.
Cook: 15 min. + releasing
Makes: 6 servings

- 2 **medium onions, thinly sliced**
- 1 **broiler/fryer chicken (3 to 4 lbs.), cut up and skin removed**
- 2 **garlic cloves, minced**
- 1 **to 2 tsp. dried oregano**
- 1 **tsp. salt**
- ½ **tsp. dried basil**
- ¼ **tsp. pepper**
- 1 **bay leaf**
- 1 **can (14½ oz.) diced tomatoes, undrained**
- 1 **can (8 oz.) tomato sauce**
- 1 **can (4 oz.) mushroom stems and pieces, drained**
- ¼ **cup white wine or water**
  Hot cooked pasta

Place onions in a 6-qt. electric pressure cooker. Add the next 11 ingredients. Lock lid; make sure vent is closed. Select manual setting; adjust pressure to high and set time for 15 minutes. When finished cooking, allow pressure to naturally release for 10 minutes, then quick-release any remaining pressure according to manufacturer's directions. Discard bay leaf. Serve chicken with sauce over pasta.

1 SERVING: 207 cal., 6g fat (2g sat. fat), 73mg chol., 787mg sod., 11g carb. (6g sugars, 3g fiber), 27g pro.

WHY YOU'LL LOVE IT...

"You would've thought I was a chef—I got raves from everyone. They just loved it. Thank you for a great recipe. They are already asking for it again. Hope you all enjoy it as much as we did."
—KATHYCOOKS1943, TASTEOFHOME.COM

CHICKEN MOLE

If you're not familiar with mole, don't be afraid of this versatile Mexican sauce. I love sharing the recipe because it's the perfect dish to experiment with.
—Darlene Morris, Franklinton, LA

Prep: 25 min.
Cook: 15 min. + releasing
Makes: 12 servings

- 2 **cups water**
- 12 **bone-in chicken thighs, skin removed (about 4½ lbs.)**
- 1 **tsp. salt**

MOLE SAUCE

- 1 **can (28 oz.) whole tomatoes, undrained**
- 1 **medium onion, chopped**
- 2 **dried ancho chilies, stems and seeds removed**
- ½ **cup sliced almonds, toasted**
- ¼ **cup raisins**
- 3 **Tbsp. olive oil**
- 2 **Tbsp. baking cocoa**
- 1 **chipotle pepper in adobo sauce**
- 3 **garlic cloves, peeled and halved**
- ¾ **tsp. ground cumin**
- ½ **tsp. ground cinnamon**
- 3 **oz. bittersweet chocolate, chopped Fresh cilantro leaves, optional**

1. Pour water into a 6-qt. electric pressure cooker. Sprinkle chicken with salt; place over water. Combine the tomatoes, onion, chilies, almonds, raisins, oil, cocoa, chipotle pepper, garlic, cumin and cinnamon in a food processor; cover and process until blended. Pour over chicken. Lock lid; make sure vent is closed. Select manual setting; adjust pressure to high and set time for 15 minutes.

2. When finished cooking, allow pressure to naturally release for 10 minutes and then quick-release any remaining pressure according to manufacturer's instructions. Remove chicken; keep warm. Skim fat from cooking liquid. Stir in chocolate until melted. Serve chicken with sauce. Sprinkle with cilantro if desired.

1 SERVING: 311 cal., 18g fat (5g sat. fat), 86mg chol., 378mg sod., 12g carb. (7g sugars, 3g fiber), 26g pro.

MANGO-PINEAPPLE CHICKEN TACOS

I lived in the Caribbean when I was a child. Every time I make this yummy chicken, the flavors of the fresh tropical fruits transport me back to those happy times.
—Lissa Nelson, Provo, UT

Prep: 25 min.
Cook: 10 min. + releasing
Makes: 16 servings

- 2 **medium mangoes, peeled and chopped**
- 1½ **cups cubed fresh pineapple or canned pineapple chunks, drained**
- 2 **medium tomatoes, chopped**
- 1 **medium red onion, finely chopped**
- 2 **small Anaheim peppers, seeded and chopped**
- 2 **green onions, finely chopped**
- 1 **Tbsp. lime juice**
- 1 **tsp. sugar**
- 4 **lbs. bone-in chicken breast halves, skin removed**
- 3 **tsp. salt**
- ¼ **cup packed brown sugar**
- 32 **taco shells, warmed**
- ¼ **cup minced fresh cilantro**

1. In a large bowl, combine the first eight ingredients. Place chicken in a 6-qt. electric pressure cooker; sprinkle with salt and brown sugar. Top with mango mixture. Lock lid; make sure vent is closed. Select manual setting; adjust pressure to high and set time for 10 minutes.

2. When finished cooking, allow pressure to naturally release for 10 minutes and then quick-release any remaining pressure according to manufacturer's instructions. Remove chicken; cool slightly. Strain cooking juices, reserving mango mixture and ½ cup juices. Discard remaining juices. When cool enough to handle, remove chicken from bones; discard bones. Shred chicken with two forks.

3. Select saute setting and adjust for high heat. Return chicken and reserved mango mixture and cooking juices to pressure cooker; stir to heat through. Serve in taco shells; sprinkle with cilantro.

1 SERVING: 246 cal., 7g fat (2g sat. fat), 51mg chol., 582mg sod., 25g carb. (10g sugars, 2g fiber), 21g pro.

FORGOTTEN JAMBALAYA

When the weather turns cool, I fix this jambalaya regularly. It's so easy…just chop the vegetables, dump everything in the pressure cooker and you're set! Even my sons, who are picky about spicy things, like this dish.
—Cindi Coss, Coppell, TX

Prep: 35 min.
Cook: 15 min.
Makes: 11 servings

1 can (14½ oz.) diced tomatoes, undrained
1 can beef broth or chicken broth (14½ oz.)
1 can (6 oz.) tomato paste
3 celery ribs, chopped
2 medium green peppers, chopped
1 medium onion, chopped
5 garlic cloves, minced
3 tsp. dried parsley flakes
2 tsp. dried basil
1½ tsp. dried oregano
1¼ tsp. salt
½ tsp. cayenne pepper
½ tsp. hot pepper sauce
1 lb. boneless skinless chicken breasts, cut into 1-in. cubes
1 lb. smoked sausage, halved and cut into ¼-in. slices
½ lb. uncooked shrimp (41-50 per lb.), peeled and deveined
Hot cooked rice

1. In a 6-qt. electric pressure cooker, combine tomatoes, broth and tomato paste. Stir in the celery, green peppers, onion, garlic and seasonings. Stir in chicken and sausage.

2. Lock lid; make sure vent is closed. Select manual setting; adjust pressure to high and set time for 8 minutes. When finished cooking, quick release pressure according to manufacturer's instructions.

3. Select saute setting and adjust for high heat. Stir in the shrimp. Cook 5 minutes longer or until shrimp turn pink. Serve with rice.

1 SERVING: 230 cal., 13g fat (5g sat. fat), 75mg chol., 1016mg sod., 9g carb. (5g sugars, 2g fiber), 20g pro.

HARVEST CHICKEN WITH WALNUT GREMOLATA

My original recipe is based on a classic veal or lamb dish but made more simply with today's hottest appliance. To lighten it up, I remove the skin and excess fat from the chicken legs. It's an elegant, complete dinner that always gets compliments.
—Patricia Harmon, Baden, PA

Prep: 25 min.
Cook: 20 min.
Makes: 6 servings

- 1 medium butternut squash (about 3 lbs.), peeled and cubed
- 1 can (14½ oz.) diced tomatoes, undrained
- 1 medium onion, chopped
- 1 celery rib, chopped
- ½ cup reduced-sodium chicken broth
- ¼ cup white wine or additional reduced-sodium chicken broth
- 1 garlic clove, minced
- 1 tsp. Italian seasoning
- ¼ tsp. coarsely ground pepper, divided
- ¼ cup all-purpose flour
- 1 tsp. seasoned salt
- 6 chicken drumsticks, skin removed
- 1 cup uncooked orzo pasta
  GREMOLATA
- 2 Tbsp. finely chopped walnuts
- 2 Tbsp. minced fresh parsley
- 1 garlic clove, minced
- 1 tsp. grated lemon peel

1. In a 6-qt. electric pressure cooker, combine the squash, tomatoes, onion, celery, broth, wine, garlic, Italian seasoning, and ⅛ tsp. pepper.

2. In a large resealable plastic bag, combine the flour, seasoned salt and remaining pepper. Add chicken, a few pieces at a time, and shake to coat. Place chicken on top of the vegetables. Lock lid; make sure vent is closed. Select manual setting; adjust pressure to high and set time for 12 minutes. When finished cooking, quick-release pressure according to manufacturer's instructions. Remove chicken and keep warm.

3. Select saute setting and adjust for high heat. Stir in orzo. Cook 7-8 minutes longer or until orzo is tender. Meanwhile, in a small bowl, combine gremolata ingredients.

4. Transfer vegetable mixture to a serving platter; top with chicken. Sprinkle with gremolata.

1 SERVING: 343 cal., 5g fat (1g sat. fat), 40mg chol., 252mg sod., 55g carb. (10g sugars, 9g fiber), 21g pro.

SWEET & TANGY CHICKEN

This dinner is hearty, delicious and fuss-free. It's the perfect entree when there's no time for significant meal prep. Most important, it's comfort food at its all-time best.
—Joan Airey, Rivers, MB

Prep: 15 min.
Cook: 20 min. + releasing
Makes: 4 servings

  1 **medium onion,**
     chopped
1½ **tsp. minced garlic**
  1 **broiler/fryer chicken**
     (3 lbs.), cut up, skin
     removed
  ⅔ **cup ketchup**
  ⅓ **cup packed brown**
     sugar
  1 **Tbsp. chili powder**
  1 **Tbsp. lemon juice**
  1 **tsp. dried basil**
  ½ **tsp. salt**
  ¼ **tsp. pepper**
  ⅛ **tsp. hot pepper sauce**
  2 **Tbsp. cornstarch**
  3 **Tbsp. cold water**

1. In a 6-qt. electric pressure cooker, combine onion and garlic; top with chicken. In a small bowl, combine the ketchup, brown sugar, chili powder, lemon juice, basil, salt, pepper and pepper sauce; pour over chicken. Lock lid; make sure vent is closed. Select manual setting; adjust pressure to high and set time for 15 minutes. When finished cooking, allow pressure to naturally release for 10 minutes and then quick-release any remaining pressure according to manufacturer's instructions. Remove chicken to a serving platter; keep warm.

2. Skim fat from cooking juices. Select saute setting and adjust for high heat; bring juices to a boil. In a small bowl, mix cornstarch and water until smooth; gradually stir into cooking juices. Cook and stir until the sauce is thickened, 1-2 minutes. Serve with chicken.

1 SERVING: 385 cal., 9g fat (3g sat. fat), 110mg chol., 892mg sod., 38g carb. (25g sugars, 2g fiber), 38g pro.

WHY YOU'LL LOVE IT...

"I thought this recipe was easy and very tasty. I left out the onion and hot pepper sauce to suit my family's taste. I will certainly make this again, especially in the summer months so I don't heat up the kitchen."

—BARRETSMOMMY, TASTEOFHOME.COM

BEEF ENTREES

Satisfy all the appetites at your table with menus starring beefy main courses. You'll find new takes on hearty classics, easy ideas that spice up taco night and tasty favorites waiting to be discovered. Dig in!

BEEF CARNITAS

I created this recipe while cleaning out my refrigerator and trying to figure out what to do with leftover pot roast. I love how simple this is. I store the rub in my cupboard to streamline preparation. What could be easier?
—Ann Piscitelli, Nokomis, FL

Prep: 40 min.
Cook: 40 min. + releasing
Makes: 16 servings plus ¼ cup leftover spice mixture

- 2 **Tbsp. kosher salt**
- 2 **Tbsp. packed brown sugar**
- 1 **Tbsp. ground cumin**
- 1 **Tbsp. smoked paprika**
- 1 **Tbsp. chili powder**
- 1 **tsp. garlic powder**
- 1 **tsp. ground mustard**
- 1 **tsp. dried oregano**
- 1 **tsp. cayenne pepper**
- 1 **(3 lbs.) boneless beef chuck roast**
- 3 **Tbsp. canola oil**
- 2 **large sweet onion, thinly sliced**
- 3 **poblano pepper, seeded and thinly sliced**
- 2 **chipotle peppers in adobo sauce, finely chopped**
- 1 **jar (16 oz.) salsa**
- 16 **flour tortillas (8 in.), warmed**
- 3 **cups crumbled queso fresco or shredded Monterey Jack cheese**
  Optional toppings: cubed avocado, sour cream and minced fresh cilantro

1. Mix the first nine ingredients. Cut roast in half; rub with ¼ cup spice mixture. Cover remaining mixture and store in a cool dry place. (Mix will keep for up to 1 year.)

2. Select saute setting on a 6-qt. electric pressure cooker and adjust for high heat; add oil. Brown roast on all sides. Place onions and peppers on meat. Top with salsa. Lock lid; make sure vent is closed. Select manual setting; adjust pressure to high and set time for 40 minutes.

3. When finished cooking, allow pressure to naturally release for 10 minutes and then quick-release any remaining pressure according to manufacturer's instructions. Remove roast; shred with two forks. Skim fat from cooking juices. Return meat to pressure cooker; heat through.

4. Using a slotted spoon, place ½ cup meat mixture on each tortilla. Sprinkle with cheese. Add toppings of your choice.

1 SERVING: 415 cal., 18g fat (6g sat. fat), 70mg chol., 830mg sod., 35g carb. (5g sugars, 1g fiber), 27g pro.

BARBECUED BEEF RIBS

Featuring a rich, tangy sauce, these tender ribs are a cinch to make. They're great for potlucks, parties and picnics where I don't want to be tied to the stove or grill.
—Erin Glass, White Hall, MD

Prep: 15 min.
Cook: 45 min. + releasing
Makes: 8 servings

- 2 Tbsp. canola oil
- 4 lbs. bone-in beef short ribs, trimmed
- 1 large sweet onion, halved and sliced
- ½ cup water
- 1 bottle (12 oz.) chili sauce
- ¾ cup plum preserves or preserves of your choice
- 2 Tbsp. packed brown sugar
- 2 Tbsp. red wine vinegar
- 2 Tbsp. Worcestershire sauce
- 2 Tbsp. Dijon mustard
- ¼ tsp. ground cloves

1. Select saute setting on a 6-qt. electric pressure cooker and adjust for high heat; add oil. Brown ribs in batches, adding additional oil as needed. Remove ribs. Brown onions. Add ribs back to the pressure cooker. Add water. Lock lid; make sure vent is closed. Select manual setting; adjust pressure to high and set time for 40 minutes. When finished cooking, allow pressure to naturally release for 10 minutes and then quick-release any remaining pressure according to the manufacturer's instructions.

2. In a small saucepan, combine remaining ingredients; cook and stir over medium heat until heated through. Remove ribs from pressure cooker; discard cooking juices. Return ribs to pressure cooker. Pour sauce over top. Lock lid; make sure vent is closed. Select manual setting; adjust pressure to low and set time for 5 minutes. When finished cooking, allow pressure to naturally release for 5 minutes and then quick-release any remaining pressure according to manufacturer's instructions. Serve ribs with sauce.

1 SERVING: 359 cal., 14g fat (5g sat. fat), 55mg chol., 860mg sod., 40g carb. (33g sugars, 0 fiber), 18g pro.

WHY YOU'LL LOVE IT...

"This dish is my family's favorite. Every time my grandmother comes to visit she asks me to make these ribs."
—CRISMILDA, TASTEOFHOME.COM

THAI COCONUT BEEF

My husband and I love Thai food, but going out on weeknights can be challenging with busy schedules. I wanted to create a Thai-inspired dinner we could also enjoy for lunch the next day. This was the mouthwatering result. Try it with chicken or pork, too.
—Ashley Lecker, Green Bay, WI

Prep: 30 min.
Cook: 40 min. + releasing
Makes: 10 servings

- 1 **boneless beef chuck roast (3 lbs.), halved**
- 1 **tsp. salt**
- 1 **tsp. pepper**
- 2 **Tbsp. canola oil**
- 1 **large sweet red pepper, sliced**
- 1 **can (13.66 oz.) coconut milk**
- ¾ **cup beef stock**
- ½ **cup creamy peanut butter**
- ¼ **cup red curry paste**
- 2 **Tbsp. soy sauce**
- 2 **Tbsp. honey**
- 2 **tsp. minced fresh gingerroot**
- ½ **lb. fresh sugar snap peas, trimmed**
- ¼ **cup minced fresh cilantro**
  Hot cooked brown or white rice
  Optional toppings: thinly sliced green onions, chopped unsalted peanuts, hot sauce and lime wedges

1. Sprinkle beef with salt and pepper. Select saute setting on a 6-qt. electric pressure cooker and adjust for high heat. Add oil; add one roast half. Brown on all sides, about 5 minutes. Remove; repeat with remaining beef.

2. Return beef to pressure cooker; add red pepper. In a bowl, whisk coconut milk with next six ingredients; pour over meat. Lock lid; make sure vent is closed. Select manual setting; adjust pressure to high, and set time for 35 minutes. When finished cooking, quick-release pressure according to manufacturer's directions. Add sugar snap peas; return to full pressure, and cook 5 minutes. Naturally release pressure for 10 minutes, then quick-release any remaining pressure.

3. Remove beef; cool slightly. Skim fat from cooking juices. Shred beef with two forks. Stir in cilantro. Serve with rice and toppings of your choice.

FREEZE OPTION: Place cooled meat mixture in freezer containers. To use, partially thaw in refrigerator overnight. Microwave, covered, on high in a microwave-safe dish until heated through, gently stirring and adding a little broth or water if necessary.

1 CUP: 421 cal., 28g fat (14g sat. fat), 88mg chol., 731mg sod., 12g carb. (7g sugars, 2g fiber), 32g pro.

TEST KITCHEN TIP
Red curry paste, a combination of Asian spices such as lemongrass and lime leaves, is an easy way to punch up the flavor of most dishes. Look for it in the ethnic aisle of your grocery store.

SAUSAGE-STUFFED FLANK STEAK

This rich and hearty entree is perfect for entertaining but easy enough for weeknight meals with the family. Give it a try tonight.
—Julie Merriman, Seattle, WA

Prep: 40 min. + standing
Cook: 15 min. + releasing
Makes: 4 servings

¾ **cup dry red wine or beef broth, divided**
¼ **cup dried cherries, coarsely chopped**
1 **beef flank steak (1½ lbs.)**
½ **tsp. salt**
½ **tsp. pepper, divided**
3 **Tbsp. olive oil, divided**
1 **medium onion, finely chopped**
4 **garlic cloves, minced**
½ **cup seasoned bread crumbs**
¼ **cup pitted Greek olives, coarsely chopped**
¼ **cup grated Parmesan cheese**
¼ **cup minced fresh basil**
½ **lb. bulk hot Italian sausage**
1 **jar (24 oz.) marinara sauce**
Hot cooked noodles

1. Combine ¼ cup wine with cherries; let stand 10 minutes. Meanwhile, cut steak into four serving-size pieces; pound with a meat mallet to ¼-in. thickness. Using ½ tsp. salt and ¼ tsp. pepper, season both sides.

2. Select saute setting on a 6-qt. electric pressure cooker and adjust for high heat. Add 1 Tbsp. oil; cook onion until tender. Add garlic; cook 1 minute longer. Transfer to a large bowl; stir in bread crumbs, olives, cheese, basil, cherry mixture and remaining pepper. Crumble sausage over bread crumb mixture; mix well.

3. Divide the sausage mixture into four portions; spread evenly over each steak piece. Roll up steaks jelly-roll style, starting with a long side; tie with kitchen string.

4. Select saute setting and adjust for high heat. Add remaining oil; brown meat on all sides. Top with marinara sauce and remaining wine. Lock lid; make sure vent is closed. Select manual setting; adjust pressure to high and set time for 15 minutes. When finished cooking, allow pressure to naturally release for 10 minutes, then quick-release any remaining pressure according to manufacturer's directions. Serve with pasta.

1 SERVING: 758 cal., 45g fat (13g sat. fat), 128mg chol., 2202mg sod., 39g carb. (19g sugars, 5g fiber), 48g pro.

GROUND BEEF STROGANOFF

My mother gave me this original recipe 40 years ago, and it's been updated for today's kitchen. It remains a wonderfully tasty dish to share around the dinner table.
—Sue Mims, Macclenny, FL

Prep: 25 min.
Cook: 20 min.
Makes: 8 servings

2 lbs. ground beef
1½ tsp. salt
1 tsp. pepper
1 Tbsp. butter
½ lb. sliced fresh mushrooms
2 medium onions, chopped
2 garlic cloves, minced
1 can (10½ oz.) condensed beef consomme, undiluted
⅓ cup all-purpose flour
2 Tbsp. tomato paste
1½ cups sour cream
Hot cooked noodles

1. Select saute setting on a 6-qt. electric pressure cooker and adjust for high heat. Add half of ground beef, salt and pepper. Cook and stir, crumbling meat, until no longer pink, 6-8 minutes. Remove meat; drain any liquid from pressure cooker. Repeat with remaining ground beef, salt and pepper.

2. Add butter, mushrooms and onions to pressure cooker; saute until onions are tender and mushrooms have released their liquid and are beginning to brown, 6-8 minutes. Add garlic; cook 1 minute longer. Return meat to cooker.

3. Lock lid; make sure vent is closed. Select manual setting; adjust pressure to high and set time for 5 minutes. When finished cooking, quick-release pressure according to manufacturer's directions.

4. Select saute setting and adjust for normal heat. In a small bowl, whisk together consomme, flour and tomato paste. Pour over meat mixture; stir to combine. Cook and stir until thickened. Stir in sour cream; cook until heated through. Serve with noodles.

1 SERVING: 357 cal., 22g fat (11g sat. fat), 104mg chol., 802mg sod., 10g carb. (4g sugars, 1g fiber), 25g pro.

TEST KITCHEN TIP
Beef consomme is similar to beef broth but made from roasted bones, vegetables and herbs. You'll find canned beef consomme in your supermarket's soup aisle.

SHORT RIBS

These short ribs explode with flavor, and they're so tender. A quick and easy alternative to traditionally braised short ribs, they are great with noodles or rice.
—Rebekah Beyer, Sabetha, KS

Prep: 30 min.
Cook: 50 min.
Makes: 6 servings

- 3 lbs. bone-in beef short ribs
- ½ tsp. salt
- ½ tsp. pepper
- 1 Tbsp. canola oil
- 2 large onions, cut into ½-in. wedges
- 6 garlic cloves, minced
- 1 Tbsp. tomato paste
- 1 cup beef broth
- 2 cups dry red wine or beef broth
- 4 fresh thyme sprigs
- 1 bay leaf
- 4 medium carrots, cut into 1-in. pieces
- 4 tsp. cornstarch
- 3 Tbsp. cold water
  Additional salt and pepper, optional

1. Sprinkle ribs with salt and pepper. Select saute setting on a 6-qt. electric pressure cooker and adjust for high heat. Add oil. Working in batches, brown ribs on all sides; transfer to a plate and keep warm.

2. Add onions to cooker; cook and stir until tender, 8-9 minutes. Add garlic and tomato paste; cook and stir 1 minute more. Stir in beef broth, wine, thyme and bay leaf. Bring to a boil; cook 8-10 minutes or until liquid is reduced by half. Add ribs back to cooker, partially but not fully submerging them. Lock lid in place; make sure vent is closed. Select manual setting; adjust pressure to high and set time for 40 minutes. When finished cooking, quick-release pressure according to manufacturer's directions. Add carrots; bring back to full pressure and cook 7 minutes. Quick-release pressure according to manufacturer's directions.

3. Remove ribs and vegetables; keep warm. Skim fat from cooking liquid. Discard thyme and bay leaf. Select saute setting and adjust for high heat; bring cooking juices to a boil. In a small bowl, mix cornstarch and water until smooth; stir into juices. Return to a boil; cook and stir until thickened, 1-2 minutes. If desired, sprinkle with the additional salt and pepper. Serve with ribs and vegetables.

1 SERVING: 250 cal., 13g fat (5g sat. fat), 55mg chol., 412mg sod., 12g carb. (4g sugars, 2g fiber), 20g pro.

TEST KITCHEN TIP
When using an all-in-one cooker, try to cut any vegetables in uniform sizes to ensure even cooking.

FAVORITE PEPPER STEAK

Pepper steak is one of my preferred dishes but I was often disappointed with how tough the beef could get. This recipe solves that problem! I've stored leftovers in one big resealable bag for another dinner, and in individual freezer containers for quick lunches.
—Julie Rhine, Zelienople, PA

Prep: 15 min.
Cook: 1 hour
Makes: 12 servings

- 1 **beef top round roast (3 lbs.)**
- 1 **cup water, divided**
- ½ **cup reduced-sodium soy sauce**
- 4 **garlic cloves, minced**
- 1 **large onion, halved and sliced**
- 1 **large green pepper, cut into ½-in. strips**
- 1 **large sweet red pepper, cut into ½-in. strips**
- ⅓ **cup cornstarch**
- 2 **tsp. sugar**
- 2 **tsp. ground ginger**
- 8 **cups hot cooked brown rice**

1. In a 6-qt. electric pressure cooker, combine roast, ½ cup water, soy sauce and garlic. Lock lid; make sure vent is closed. Select manual setting; adjust pressure to high and set time for 1 hour. When finished cooking, quick-release pressure according to manufacturer's directions. Add onion and peppers. Lock lid; make sure vent is closed. Select manual setting; adjust pressure to high and set time for 2 minutes. When finished cooking, quick-release pressure. Remove beef to a cutting board.

2. Select saute setting and adjust for high heat; bring liquid to a boil. In a small bowl, mix cornstarch, sugar, ginger and remaining water until smooth; gradually stir into vegetable mixture. Cook and stir until sauce is thickened, 1-2 minutes.

3. Cut beef into slices. Stir gently into sauce; heat through. Serve with rice.

FREEZE OPTION: Freeze cooled beef mixture in freezer containers. To use, partially thaw in refrigerator overnight. Heat through in a saucepan, stirring occasionally and adding a little water if necessary.

1 SERVING: 343 cal., 5g fat (2g sat. fat), 63mg chol., 422mg sod., 42g carb. (2g sugars, 3g fiber), 30g pro. **DIABETIC EXCHANGES:** 3 starch, 3 lean meat.

CUBAN ROPA VIEJA

This recipe brings authentic Cuban flavors to your home. I love having this as a go-to recipe for a tasty weeknight meal.
—Melissa Pelkey Hass, Waleska, GA

Prep: 25 min.
Cook: 20 min. + releasing
Makes: 8 servings

- 6 bacon strips, chopped
- 2 beef flank steak (1 lb. each), cut in half
- 1 can (28 oz.) crushed tomatoes
- 2 cups beef stock
- 1 can (6 oz.) tomato paste
- 5 garlic cloves, minced
- 1 Tbsp. ground cumin
- 2 tsp. dried thyme
- ¾ tsp. salt
- ½ tsp. pepper
- 1 medium onion, thinly sliced
- 1 medium sweet pepper, sliced
- 1 medium green pepper, sliced
- ¼ cup minced fresh cilantro
  Hot cooked rice

1. Select saute setting on a 6-qt. electric pressure cooker and adjust for high heat; add bacon. Cook bacon until crisp, stirring occasionally. Remove bacon with a slotted spoon; drain on paper towels.

2. In drippings, brown steak in batches. Return bacon to pressure cooker. In a large bowl, combine tomatoes, beef stock, tomato paste, garlic, seasonings, onions and peppers; pour over meat. Lock lid; make sure vent is closed. Select manual setting; adjust pressure to high and set time for 12 minutes. When finished cooking, allow pressure to naturally release for 10 minutes and then quick-release any remaining pressure according to manufacturer's instructions.

3. Shred beef with two forks; return to pressure cooker. Stir in cilantro. Remove with a slotted spoon; serve with rice.

1 SERVING: 335 cal., 17g fat (6g sat. fat), 68mg chol., 765mg sod., 17g carb. (9g sugars, 4g fiber), 29g pro.

POT ROAST HASH

I love to cook a Sunday-style pot roast on a weeknight. Here's a fun take on the all-time favorite that works well any day of the week.
—Gina Jackson, Ogdensburg, NY

Prep: 20 min.
Cook: 45 min. + releasing
Makes: 10 servings

- 1 **cup warm water (110° to 115°)**
- 1 **Tbsp. beef base**
- ½ **lb. sliced fresh mushrooms**
- 1 **large onion, coarsely chopped**
- 3 **garlic cloves, minced**
- 1 **boneless beef chuck roast (3 lbs.)**
- ½ **tsp. pepper**
- 1 **Tbsp. Worcestershire sauce**
- 1 **pkg. (28 oz.) frozen O'Brien potatoes**

EGGS
- 2 **Tbsp. butter, divided**
- 10 **large eggs, divided**
- ½ **tsp. salt, divided**
- ½ **tsp. pepper, divided**
 Minced chives

1. In a 6-qt. electric pressure cooker, whisk water and beef base; add mushrooms, onion and garlic. Sprinkle the roast with pepper; transfer all to pressure cooker. Drizzle with the Worcestershire sauce. Lock lid; make sure vent is closed. Select manual setting; adjust pressure to high and set time for 45 minutes. When finished cooking, allow pressure to naturally release for 10 minutes, then quick-release any remaining pressure according to manufacturer's directions.

2. Remove roast; when cool enough to handle, shred meat with two forks. In a large skillet, cook potatoes according to package directions; stir in shredded beef. Using a slotted spoon, transfer vegetables from pressure cooker to skillet; heat through. Discard cooking juices.

3. For eggs, heat 1 Tbsp. butter over medium-high heat in another large skillet. Break five eggs, one at a time, into pan. Sprinkle with half the salt and pepper. Reduce heat to low. Cook until eggs reach desired doneness, turning after whites are set if desired. Repeat with remaining butter, eggs, salt and pepper. Serve eggs over hash; sprinkle with chives.

1 SERVING: 429 cal., 24g fat (8g sat. fat), 281mg chol., 15mg sod., 15g carb. (2g sugars, 2g fiber), 35g pro.

TEST KITCHEN TIP
Try the flavorful meat mixture with scrambled eggs if you prefer, or save some time and simply leave out the eggs altogether.

BEEF OSSO BUCCO

This osso bucco includes a thick, savory sauce complemented by the addition of gremolata, a chopped herb condiment made of lemon zest, garlic and parsley.
—*Taste of Home* **Test Kitchen**

Prep: 45 min.
Cook: 40 min./batch
  + releasing
Makes: 6 servings

- ½ **cup all-purpose flour**
- ¾ **tsp. salt, divided**
- ½ **tsp. pepper**
- 6 **beef shanks (14 oz. each)**
- 2 **Tbsp. butter**
- 1 **Tbsp. olive oil**
- ½ **cup white wine or beef broth**
- 1 **can (14½ oz.) diced tomatoes, undrained**
- 1½ **cups beef broth**
- 2 **medium carrots, chopped**
- 1 **medium onion, chopped**
- 1 **celery rib, sliced**
- 1 **tsp. dried thyme**
- 1 **tsp. dried oregano**
- 2 **bay leaves**
- 2 **Tbsp. cornstarch**
- ¼ **cup cold water**

GREMOLATA

- ⅓ **cup minced fresh parsley**
- 1 **Tbsp. grated lemon zest**
- 1 **Tbsp. grated orange zest**
- 2 **garlic cloves, minced**

1. In a large resealable plastic bag, combine flour, ½ tsp. salt and pepper. Pat beef dry with paper towels. Add beef to bag, a couple pieces at a time; shake to coat.

2. In a 6-qt. electric pressure cooker, select saute setting and adjust for high heat. Add 1 Tbsp. butter and 1½ tsp. oil; brown three beef shanks. Remove from pressure cooker; add ¼ cup wine, stirring to loosen browned bits. In a large bowl, combine tomatoes, broth, vegetables, seasonings and remaining salt. Return browned beef shanks to cooker; pour in half of tomato mixture.

3. Lock lid; make sure vent is closed. Select manual setting; adjust pressure to high and set time for 40 minutes. When finished cooking, allow pressure to naturally release for 10 minutes, then quick-release any remaining pressure according to manufacturer's directions. Remove meat and vegetables from pressure cooker; keep warm. Make second batch with remaining ingredients, repeating previous procedure.

4. After removing all meat and vegetables, discard bay leaves. Skim fat from cooking juices. Select saute setting and adjust for high heat. Bring to a boil. In a small bowl, mix cornstarch and water until smooth; stir into cooking juices. Return to a boil, stirring constantly; cook and stir until thickened, about 2 minutes.

5. In a small bowl, combine gremolata ingredients. Serve beef with gremolata and sauce.

1 SERVING: 398 cal., 15g fat (6g sat. fat), 112mg chol., 640mg sod., 17g carb. (5g sugars, 4g fiber), 47g pro.

BEEF BRISKET IN BEER

One bite of this super tender brisket, and your family will be hooked! The rich gravy is perfect for spooning over a side of creamy mashed potatoes.
—Eunice Stoen, Decorah, IA

Prep: 15 min.
Cook: 70 min. + releasing
Makes: 6 servings

- 1 **fresh beef brisket (2½ to 3 lbs.)**
- 2 **tsp. liquid smoke, optional**
- 1 **tsp. celery salt**
- ½ **tsp. pepper**
- ¼ **tsp. salt**
- 1 **large onion, sliced**
- 1 **can (12 oz.) beer or nonalcoholic beer**
- 2 **tsp. Worcestershire sauce**
- 2 **Tbsp. cornstarch**
- ¼ **cup cold water**

1. Cut brisket in half; rub with liquid smoke, if desired, along with celery salt, pepper and salt. Place brisket fatty side up in a 6-qt. electric pressure cooker. Top with onion. Combine beer and Worcestershire sauce; pour over meat. Lock lid; make sure vent is closed. Select manual setting; adjust pressure to high and set time for 70 minutes. When finished cooking, allow pressure to naturally release for 10 minutes, then quick-release any remaining pressure according to manufacturer's directions. If brisket isn't fork-tender, reseal cooker and cook for an additional 10-15 minutes.

2. Remove brisket; cover with foil and keep warm. Strain cooking juices; return juices to pressure cooker. Select saute setting and adjust for high heat; bring liquid to a boil. In a small bowl, mix cornstarch and water until smooth; gradually stir into juices. Cook and stir until sauce is thickened, about 2 minutes. Serve with beef.

1 SERVING: 285 cal., 8g fat (3g sat. fat), 80mg chol., 430mg sod., 7g carb. (3g sugars, 0 fiber), 39g pro.

TEST KITCHEN TIP
Liquid smoke is a great addition to this recipe as it adds depth of flavor. Be careful not to overdo it, though; a small amount goes a long way. Look for liquid smoke near the spices and marinades in your grocery store.

BOEUF BOURGUIGNON

I've wanted to make beef Burgundy ever since I got one of Julia Child's cookbooks, but I wanted to find a way to fix it easily. My version of the popular beef stew is still rich, hearty and delicious, but without the need to watch it on the stovetop or in the oven.
—Crystal Jo Bruns, Iliff, CO

Prep: 30 min. + marinating
Cook: 30 min. + releasing
Makes: 12 servings

    3 lbs. beef stew meat
1¾ cups dry red wine
    3 Tbsp. olive oil
    3 Tbsp. dried minced
       onion
    2 Tbsp. dried parsley
       flakes
    1 bay leaf
    1 tsp. dried thyme
   ¼ tsp. pepper
    8 bacon strips, chopped
    1 lb. whole fresh
       mushrooms, quartered
  24 pearl onions, peeled
       (about 2 cups)
    2 garlic cloves, minced
   ⅓ cup all-purpose flour
    1 tsp. salt
       Hot cooked whole
         wheat egg noodles,
         optional

1. Place beef in a large resealable plastic bag; add wine, oil and seasonings. Seal bag and turn to coat. Refrigerate overnight.

2. Select saute setting on a 6-qt. electric pressure cooker and adjust for high heat. Add bacon; cook until crisp, stirring occasionally. Remove with a slotted spoon; drain on paper towels. Discard drippings, reserving 1 Tbsp. in pressure cooker.

3. Add mushrooms and onions to drippings; cook and stir until tender. Add garlic; cook 1 minute longer.

4. Drain beef, reserving marinade. Add beef to pressure cooker. Sprinkle beef with flour and salt; toss to coat. Top with bacon and mushroom mixture. Add reserved marinade.

5. Lock lid; make sure vent is closed. Select manual setting; adjust pressure to high and set time for 20 minutes. When finished cooking, allow pressure to naturally release for 10 minutes and then quick-release any remaining pressure according to manufacturer's instructions.

6. Select saute setting and adjust for high heat; bring liquid to a boil. Cook 15-20 minutes or until sauce reaches desired thickness. Remove bay leaf. If desired, serve the stew with hot noodles.

⅔ **CUP:** 289 cal., 15g fat (5g sat. fat), 77mg chol., 350mg sod., 8g carb. (2g sugars, 1g fiber), 25g pro.

BEEF TIPS

These beef tips remind me of a childhood favorite. I cook them with mushrooms and serve it all over brown rice, noodles or mashed potatoes.
—Amy Lents, Grand Forks, ND

Prep: 20 min.
Cook: 15 min.
Makes: 4 servings

3 tsp. olive oil
1 beef top sirloin steak (1 lb.), cubed
½ tsp. salt
¼ tsp. pepper
⅓ cup dry red wine or beef broth
½ lb. sliced baby portobello mushrooms
1 small onion, halved and sliced
2 cups beef broth
1 Tbsp. Worcestershire sauce
3 to 4 Tbsp. cornstarch
¼ cup cold water
   Hot cooked mashed potatoes

1. Select saute setting on a 6-qt. electric pressure cooker and adjust for high heat. Add 2 tsp. oil. Sprinkle beef with salt and pepper. Brown meat in batches, adding oil as needed. Transfer meat to a bowl. Add the wine to cooker, stirring to loosen browned bits. Return beef to cooker; add mushrooms, onion, broth and Worcestershire sauce. Lock lid; make sure vent is closed. Select manual setting; adjust pressure to high and set time for 15 minutes. When finished cooking, quick-release pressure according to manufacturer's directions.

2. Select saute setting and adjust for high heat; bring liquid to a boil. In a small bowl, mix cornstarch and water until smooth; gradually stir into beef mixture. Cook and stir until sauce is thickened, 1-2 minutes. Serve with mashed potatoes.

1 CUP: 212 cal., 7g fat (2g sat. fat), 46mg chol., 836mg sod., 8g carb. (2g sugars, 1g fiber), 27g pro. **DIABETIC EXCHANGES:** 3 lean meat, ½ starch, ½ fat.

SHREDDED BEEF BURRITOS

Beef chuck roast makes these burritos so savory and filling. Double the recipe and take the filling to your next potluck or office party and create a build-your-own burrito bar!
—Hope Wasylenki, Gahanna, OH

Prep: 20 min.
Cook: 40 min. + releasing
Makes: 6 servings

2½ lbs. boneless beef chuck roast, cut into 4 pieces
1 Tbsp. chili powder
1½ tsp. ground cumin
   Dash salt
1 Tbsp. canola oil
1 small onion, finely chopped
1 jalapeno pepper, seeded and finely chopped
1 garlic clove, minced
1 can (14½ oz.) crushed tomatoes in puree
1 cup (8 oz.) salsa verde
¼ cup beef broth
   Tortillas
   Optional toppings: shredded cheddar cheese, sour cream, guacamole, salsa and fresh cilantro leaves

1. Season the roast with chili powder, cumin and salt. Select saute setting on a 6-qt. electric pressure cooker; adjust for high heat. Add oil; brown roast on all sides. Top with onion, pepper and garlic. Add tomatoes, salsa verde and beef broth. Lock lid; make sure vent is closed. Select manual setting; adjust pressure to high and set time for 40 minutes.

2. When finished cooking, allow pressure to naturally release for 10 minutes and then quick-release any remaining pressure according to manufacturer's instructions. Remove roast; shred with two forks. Skim fat from cooking juices. Return meat to pressure cooker; heat through. Wrap beef in tortillas with adding toppings as desired.

FREEZE OPTION: Freeze cooled beef mixture in freezer containers. To use, thaw in refrigerator overnight. Heat through in a saucepan, stirring occasionally.

1 BURRITO: 380 cal., 21g fat (7g sat. fat), 123mg chol., 553mg sod., 10g carb. (5g sugars, 2g fiber), 39g pro.

FRENCH DIP SANDWICHES

Beef chuck roast gives this classic sandwich a savory flavor. Add a salad or fries and you have a terrific meal. This is also a great make-ahead recipe that can be prepared a few days before serving and stored in the refrigerator.
—*Taste of Home* Test Kitchen

Prep: 20 min.
Cook: 1 hour + releasing
Makes: 10 servings

- 1 **boneless beef chuck roast (about 3 lbs.)**
- 1 **tsp. dried oregano**
- 1 **tsp. dried rosemary, crushed**
- ½ **tsp. seasoned salt**
- ¼ **tsp. pepper**
- 3 **cups beef broth**
- 1 **bay leaf**
- 1 **garlic clove, peeled**
  French bread, sliced

1. Place roast on a rack in an electric pressure cooker; sprinkle with oregano, rosemary, seasoned salt and pepper. Add broth, bay leaf and garlic. Lock lid; make sure vent is closed. Select manual setting; adjust pressure to high and set time for 75 minutes.

2. When finished cooking, allow pressure to naturally release for 10 minutes, then quick-release any remaining pressure according to the manufacturer's directions. Remove beef; shred with two forks. Discard bay leaf and garlic from broth. Serve shredded beef on French bread with broth for dipping.

1 SANDWICH: 237 cal., 13g fat (5g sat. fat), 88mg chol., 378mg sod., 1g carb. (0 sugars, 0 fiber), 27g pro.

SOUPS & SANDWICHES

Your all-in-one cooker does double duty with these popular recipes. Whether serving a heartwarming soup, comforting sammie or a meal of both, you'll double up on flavor with any of these family faves.

POTATO SOUP

I decided to give some character to basic potato chowder by adding roasted red peppers. The extra flavor gives a deliciously unique twist to an otherwise ordinary soup.
—Mary Shivers, Ada, OK

Prep: 20 min.
Cook: 25 min.
Makes: 12 servings (3 qt.)

- 3 **lbs. potatoes, peeled and cut into ½-in. cubes (about 8 cups)**
- 1 **large onion, chopped**
- 1 **jar (7 oz.) roasted sweet red peppers, drained and chopped**
- 1 **small celery rib, chopped**
- 6 **cups chicken broth**
- ½ **tsp. garlic powder**
- ½ **tsp. seasoned salt**
- ½ **tsp. pepper**
- ⅛ **tsp. rubbed sage**
- ⅓ **cup all-purpose flour**
- 2 **cups heavy whipping cream, divided**
- 1 **cup grated Parmesan cheese, divided**
- 8 **bacon strips, cooked and crumbled**
- 2 **Tbsp. minced fresh cilantro**

1. Place first nine ingredients in a 6-qt. electric pressure cooker. Lock lid; make sure vent is closed. Select manual setting; adjust pressure to high and set time for 15 minutes. When finished cooking, quick-release pressure according to manufacturer's directions.

2. Select saute setting and adjust for low heat. Mix flour and ½ cup cream until smooth; stir into soup. Stir in ¾ cup Parmesan cheese, bacon, cilantro and remaining cream. Cook and stir until slightly thickened, 6-8 minutes. Serve with remaining cheese.

1 CUP: 289 cal., 19g fat (11g sat. fat), 59mg chol., 848mg sod., 23g carb. (4g sugars, 1g fiber), 7g pro.

TEST KITCHEN TIP
Any combination of potatoes will work in this recipe, but russet potatoes hold up best to the heat.

ITALIAN SAUSAGE & KALE SOUP

The first time I made this colorful soup, we knew it was a keeper. The house smells incredible as the flavorful meal simmers to perfection.
—Sarah Stombaugh, Chicago, IL

Prep: 20 min.
Cook: 10 min. + releasing
Makes: 8 servings (3½ qt.)

- 1 **lb. bulk hot Italian sausage**
- 6 **cups chopped fresh kale**
- 2 **cans (15½ oz. each) great northern beans, rinsed and drained**
- 1 **can (28 oz.) crushed tomatoes**
- 4 **large carrots, finely chopped (about 3 cups)**
- 1 **medium onion, chopped**
- 3 **garlic cloves, minced**
- 1 **tsp. dried oregano**
- ¼ **tsp. salt**
- ⅛ **tsp. pepper**
- 5 **cups chicken stock**
  Grated Parmesan cheese

1. In a 6-qt. electric pressure cooker, select saute setting and adjust for high heat. Add sausage. Cook and stir, crumbling meat, until no longer pink. Remove sausage; drain. Return sausage to pressure cooker.

2. Add the next 10 ingredients. Lock lid; make sure vent is closed. Select manual setting; adjust pressure to high and set time for 10 minutes. When finished cooking, allow pressure to naturally release for 5 minutes, then quick-release any remaining pressure according to manufacturer's directions.

3. Top each serving with cheese.

1¾ **CUPS:** 297 cal., 13g fat (4g sat. fat), 31mg chol., 1105mg sod., 31g carb. (7g sugars, 9g fiber), 16g pro.

TEST KITCHEN TIP
Lighten things up a bit by substituting turkey sausage for the Italian sausage.

CAROLINA-STYLE VINEGAR BBQ CHICKEN

I live in Georgia but I certainly appreciate the tangy, sweet and slightly spicy flavor of Carolina vinegar chicken. It's a great change of pace and ready in no time.
—Ramona Parris, Canton, GA

Takes: 25 min.
Makes: 6 servings

- 2 cups water
- 1 cup white vinegar
- ¼ cup sugar
- 1 Tbsp. reduced-sodium chicken base
- 1 tsp. crushed red pepper flakes
- ¾ tsp. salt
- 1½ lbs. boneless skinless chicken breasts
- 6 whole wheat hamburger buns, split, optional

1. In a 6-qt. electric pressure cooker, mix the first six ingredients; add chicken. Lock lid; make sure vent is closed. Select manual setting; adjust pressure to high and set time for 5 minutes.

2. When finished cooking, allow pressure to naturally release for 8 minutes, then quick-release any remaining pressure according to manufacturer's directions.

3. Remove chicken; cool slightly. Reserve 1 cup of cooking juices; discard remaining juices. Shred chicken with two forks. Combine with reserved juices. If desired, serve chicken mixture on buns.

½ **CUP CHICKEN MIXTURE:** 135 cal., 3g fat (1g sat. fat), 63mg chol., 228mg sod., 3g carb. (3g sugars, 0 fiber), 23g pro. **DIABETIC EXCHANGES:** 3 lean meat.

HOMEMADE CHICKEN BROTH

There's nothing better and more satisfying than making your own chicken broth. You can control the amount of seasoning and salt, so you can customize it for whatever recipes you're using it in.
—*Taste of Home* Test Kitchen

Prep: 10 min.
Cook: 45 min. + chilling
Makes: about 6 cups

2½ lbs. bony chicken pieces
     (legs, wings, necks or
     back bones)
  2 celery ribs with leaves,
     cut into chunks
  2 medium carrots, cut
     into chunks
  2 medium onions,
     quartered
  2 bay leaves
  ½ tsp. dried rosemary,
     crushed
  ½ tsp. dried thyme
  8 to 10 whole
     peppercorns
  6 cups cold water

1. Place all ingredients in a 6-qt. electric pressure cooker. Lock lid; make sure vent is closed. Select manual; adjust pressure to high and set time for 45 minutes. When finished cooking, allow pressure to naturally release.

2. Remove chicken; set aside until cool enough to handle. Remove meat from bones. Discard bones; save meat for another use. Strain broth, discarding vegetables and seasonings. Refrigerate 8 hours or overnight. Skim any fat from the surface.

1 CUP: 25 cal., 0 fat (0 sat. fat), 0 chol., 130mg sod., 2g carb. (0 sugars, 0 fiber), 4g pro.

WHY YOU'LL LOVE IT...

"My family and I have enjoyed this recipe many times since I discovered it. Why it took me so long to make my own broth, I don't know. This was very easy!"
—MARIAN C. BROWN, TASTEOFHOME.COM

CHICKEN ENCHILADA SOUP

This soup delivers a big bowl of comfort—just ask my husband. Toppings such as chopped avocado, sour cream and tortilla strips are a must in our house.
—Heather Sewell, Harrisonville, MO

Prep: 25 min.
Cook: 20 min. + releasing
Makes: 8 servings (3¼ qt.)

- 1 **Tbsp. canola oil**
- 2 **Anaheim pepper or poblano pepper, finely chopped**
- 1 **medium onion, chopped**
- 3 **garlic cloves, minced**
- 1 **lb. boneless skinless chicken breasts**
- 1 **carton (48 oz.) chicken broth**
- 1 **can (14½ oz.) Mexican diced tomatoes, undrained**
- 1 **can (10 oz.) enchilada sauce**
- 2 **Tbsp. tomato paste**
- 1 **Tbsp. chili powder**
- 2 **tsp. ground cumin**
- ½ **tsp. pepper**
- ½ **to 1 tsp. chipotle hot pepper sauce, optional**
- ⅓ **cup minced fresh cilantro**
  Optional: shredded cheddar cheese, cubed avocado, sour cream and tortilla strips

1. Select saute setting on a 6-qt. electric pressure cooker and adjust for high heat; add oil. Add peppers and onion; cook and stir 6-8 minutes or until tender. Add garlic; cook 1 minute longer. Add the chicken, broth, tomatoes, enchilada sauce, tomato paste, seasonings and, if desired, pepper sauce. Stir. Lock lid; make sure vent is closed. Select manual setting; adjust pressure to high and set time for 8 minutes. When finished cooking, allow pressure to naturally release for 7 minutes, then quick-release any remaining pressure according to manufacturer's instructions.

2. Remove chicken from the pressure cooker. Shred with two forks; return to pressure cooker. Stir in cilantro. Serve with toppings as desired.

1 SERVING: 132 cal., 4g fat (1g sat. fat), 35mg chol., 1117mg sod., 9g carb. (4g sugars, 2g fiber), 14g pro.

CUBAN PULLED PORK SANDWICHES

I lived in Florida for a while and loved the pork served there. I went about making it for myself after I moved and here's the tasty result. The flavorful meat makes for an amazing dinner. It's great for tacos, too.
—Lacie Griffin, Austin, TX

Prep: 20 min.
Cook: 25 min. + releasing
Makes: 16 servings

- 1 boneless pork shoulder butt roast (4 to 5 lbs.)
- 2 tsp. salt
- 2 tsp. pepper
- 1 Tbsp. olive oil
- 1 cup orange juice
- ½ cup lime juice
- 12 garlic cloves, minced
- 2 Tbsp. spiced rum, optional
- 2 Tbsp. ground coriander
- 2 tsp. white pepper
- 1 tsp. cayenne pepper

SANDWICHES
- 2 loaves (1 lb. each) French bread
  Yellow mustard, optional
- 16 dill pickle slices
- 1½ lbs. thinly sliced deli ham
- 1½ lbs. Swiss cheese, sliced

1. Cut pork into 2-in.-thick pieces; season with salt and pepper. Select saute setting on a 6-qt. electric pressure cooker; adjust for high heat. Add oil; working in batches, brown pork on all sides. Remove from cooker.

2. Add orange and lime juices, stirring to scrape browned bits from bottom of cooker. Add garlic, rum, if desired, coriander, white pepper and cayenne pepper. Return pork and any collected juices to cooker. Lock lid in place; make sure vent is closed. Select manual setting; adjust pressure to high and set time for 25 minutes.

3. When finished cooking, naturally release pressure for 10 minutes, then quick-release any remaining pressure according to manufacturer's instructions. Remove roast; when cool enough to handle, shred with two forks. Remove 1 cup cooking liquid from cooker; add to pork and toss.

4. Cut each loaf of bread in half lengthwise. If desired, spread mustard over cut sides of bread. Layer bottom halves of bread with pickles, pork mixture, ham and cheese. Replace tops. Cut each loaf into eight slices.

1 SANDWICH: 573 cal., 28g fat (12g sat. fat), 126mg chol., 1240mg sod., 35g carb. (5g sugars, 2g fiber), 45g pro.

LENTIL PUMPKIN SOUP

Plenty of herbs and spices brighten up my hearty pumpkin soup. What a great way to mix up ho-hum meals on crazy weeknights.
—Laura Magee, Houlton, WI

Takes: 25 min.
Makes: 6 servings (2¼ qt.)

- 1 lb. medium red potatoes (about 4 medium), cut into ½-in. pieces
- 1 can (15 oz.) canned pumpkin
- 1 cup dried lentils, rinsed
- 1 medium onion, chopped
- 3 garlic cloves, minced
- ½ tsp. ground ginger
- ½ tsp. pepper
- ⅛ tsp. salt
- 2 cans (14½ oz. each) vegetable broth
- 1½ cups water
  Minced fresh cilantro, optional

In a 6-qt. electric pressure cooker, combine first 10 ingredients. Lock lid; make sure vent is closed. Select manual setting; adjust pressure to high and set time for 12 minutes. When finished cooking, quick-release pressure according to manufacturer's directions. If desired, sprinkle servings with cilantro.

1½ CUPS: 210 cal., 1g fat (0 sat. fat), 0 chol., 463mg sod., 42g carb. (5g sugars, 7g fiber), 11g pro. **DIABETIC EXCHANGES:** 2½ starch, 1 lean meat.

TEST KITCHEN TIP
Many family cooks agree there is little to no difference in flavor between fresh-cooked pumpkin and canned. But for most cooks, the time-saving convenience of cooking with canned pumpkin is a bonus!

PORK STEW

I make a heartwarming stew with pork ribs and hominy often. It's a fill-you-up dish of lightly spiced comfort.
—Genie Gunn, Asheville, NC

Prep: 10 min.
Cook: 25 min. + releasing
Makes: 6 servings

- 1 **can (14½ oz.) diced tomatoes, undrained**
- 1 **can (14½ oz.) diced tomatoes with mild green chilies, undrained**
- 1 **can (10 oz.) green enchilada sauce**
- 1 **medium onion, finely chopped**
- 3 **garlic cloves, minced**
- 2 **tsp. ground cumin**
- ¼ **tsp. salt**
- 1 **lb. boneless country-style pork ribs**
- 1 **can (15½ oz.) hominy, rinsed and drained**
- 2 **medium carrot, finely chopped**
  Lime wedges
  Minced fresh cilantro
  Corn tortillas (6 in.), optional

1. In a 6-qt. electric pressure cooker, combine the first seven ingredients; add pork. Lock lid; make sure vent is closed. Select manual setting; adjust pressure to high and set time for 20 minutes. When finished cooking, quick-release the pressure according to manufacturer's directions; add the hominy and carrots. Lock lid in place and cook an additional 5 minutes. Allow pressure to naturally release for 10 minutes and then quick-release any remaining pressure.

2. Remove pork from pressure cooker. Cut into bite-sized pieces; return to pressure cooker. Serve with lime wedges and cilantro and, if desired, corn tortillas.

1 SERVING: 229 cal., 8g fat (3g sat. fat), 44mg chol., 961mg sod., 23g carb. (7g sugars, 5g fiber), 15g pro.

BEER-BRAISED PULLED HAM

To jazz up leftover ham, I cook it with a no-fuss beer sauce. Buns loaded with the ham, pickles and mustard are irresistible and perfect for potlucks and large get-togethers.
—Ann Sheehy, Lawrence, MA

Prep: 10 min.
Cook: 25 min. + releasing
Makes: 16 servings

  2 **bottles (12 oz. each) beer or nonalcoholic beer**
  ¾ **cup German or Dijon mustard, divided**
  ½ **tsp. coarsely ground pepper**
  1 **fully cooked bone-in ham (4 lbs.)**
  4 **fresh rosemary sprigs**
  16 **pretzel hamburger buns, split**
      Dill pickle slices, optional

1. In a 6-qt. electric pressure cooker, whisk together beer, ½ cup mustard and pepper. Add the ham and rosemary. Lock lid; make sure vent is closed. Select manual setting; adjust pressure to high and set time for 20 minutes. When finished cooking, allow pressure to naturally release for 10 minutes, then quick-release any remaining pressure according to manufacturer's directions.

2. Remove ham; cool slightly. Discard rosemary sprigs. Skim fat from liquid remaining in pressure cooker. Select saute setting and adjust for high heat. Bring liquid to a boil; cook for 5 minutes.

3. When ham is cool enough to handle, shred meat with two forks. Discard bone. Return ham to pressure cooker; heat through. To serve, place shredded ham on pretzel bun bottoms with remaining mustard and, if desired, dill pickle slices. Replace tops.

TEST KITCHEN TIP
Create dozens of appetizers when you serve the pulled ham on slider buns instead of pretzel buns.

1 SANDWICH: 378 cal., 9g fat (1g sat. fat), 50mg chol., 1246mg sod., 50g carb. (4g sugars, 2g fiber), 25g pro.

EASY PORK POSOLE

Looking for a savory meal in a bowl? Sit down to a Mexican classic full of cubed pork, sliced sausage. hominy and more. It all goes into the electric pressure cooker, so you can enjoy dinner in a flash.
—Greg Fontenot, The Woodlands, TX

Prep: 30 min.
Cook: 10 min. + releasing
Makes: 8 servings (2 qt.)

- 1 Tbsp. canola oil
- ½ lb. boneless pork shoulder butt roast, cubed
- ½ lb. fully cooked andouille sausage links, sliced
- 2 medium tomatoes, seeded and chopped
- 1 can (15 oz.) hominy, rinsed and drained
- 1 cup minced fresh cilantro
- 1 medium onion, chopped
- 4 green onions, chopped
- 1 jalapeno pepper, seeded and chopped
- 2 garlic cloves, minced
- 1 Tbsp. chili powder
- 1 tsp. ground cumin
- ½ tsp. cayenne pepper
- ½ tsp. coarsely ground pepper
- 6 cups reduced-sodium chicken broth
  Optional ingredients: corn tortillas, chopped onion, minced fresh cilantro and lime wedges

1. In a 6-qt. electric pressure cooker, select saute setting and adjust for normal heat. Add oil. Add pork cubes and sausage. Cook and stir until browned. Remove pork and sausage; drain. Return meats to pressure cooker.

2. Add next 12 ingredients. Lock lid; make sure vent is closed. Select manual setting; adjust pressure to high and set time for 10 minutes. When finished cooking, allow pressure to naturally release for 5 minutes, then quick-release any remaining pressure according to manufacturer's directions. If desired, serve with tortillas, onion, cilantro and lime wedges.

NOTE: Wear disposable gloves when cutting hot peppers; the oils can burn skin. Avoid touching your face.

1 CUP: 190 cal., 11g fat (3g sat. fat), 54mg chol., 957mg sod., 12g carb. (2g sugars, 3g fiber), 14g pro.

TEST KITCHEN TIP
Canned hominy is dried corn that has been treated and soaked, resulting in a puffy, chewy texture. Look for hominy near the canned beans in the grocery store.

SWEETS & DESSERTS

Say what? It's true—you can prepare luscious treats in your electric pressure cooker! From cakes to cobblers, these heavenly bites make any night of the week feel like an extra-special occasion.

VERY VANILLA CHEESECAKE

Cinnamon and vanilla give this cheesecake so much flavor, and making it in the electric pressure cooker creates a silky, smooth texture that's hard to resist.
—Krista Lanphier, Milwaukee, WI

Prep: 20 min.
Cook: 65 min. + cooling
Makes: 6 servings

- 1 **cup water**
- ¾ **cup graham cracker crumbs**
- 1 **Tbsp. plus ⅔ cup sugar, divided**
- ¼ **tsp. ground cinnamon**
- 2½ **Tbsp. butter, melted**
- 2 **pkg. (8 oz. each) cream cheese, softened**
- 2 **to 3 tsp. vanilla extract**
- 2 **large eggs, lightly beaten**

TOPPING (optional)
- 4 **oz. white baking chocolate, chopped**
- 3 **Tbsp. heavy whipping cream**
  Sliced fresh strawberries or raspberries, optional

1. Grease a 6-in. springform pan; pour water into a 6-qt. electric pressure cooker.

2. Mix cracker crumbs, 1 Tbsp. sugar and cinnamon; stir in butter. Press onto bottom and about 1 in. up sides of the prepared pan.

3. In another bowl, beat cream cheese and remaining sugar until smooth. Beat in vanilla. Add eggs; beat on low speed just until combined. Pour over crust.

4. Cover cheesecake tightly with foil. Place springform pan on a trivet with handles; lower into cooker. Lock lid; make sure vent is closed. Select manual setting; adjust pressure to low and set time for 1 hour and 5 minutes. When finished cooking, quick-release the pressure. The cheesecake should be jiggly but set in center.

5. Carefully remove springform pan from pressure cooker; remove foil. Cool cheesecake on a wire rack 1 hour. Loosen sides from pan with a knife. Refrigerate overnight, covering when completely cooled.

6. For topping, melt chocolate and cream in a microwave; stir until smooth. Cool slightly. Remove rim from springform pan. Pour chocolate mixture over cheesecake. If desired, sprinkle with berries to serve.

1 SLICE: 484 cal., 34g fat (19g sat. fat), 151mg chol., 357mg sod., 39g carb. (31g sugars, 0 fiber), 8g pro.

TEST KITCHEN TIP
Find 6-inch springform pans at Wilton Industries. Visit *wilton.com* or call 800-794-5866.

MAPLE CREME BRULEE

The pressure cooker is the perfect way to prepare classic creme brulee. The crunchy brown sugar topping in this recipe is wonderful, and the custard is smooth and creamy.
—*Taste of Home* Test Kitchen

Prep: 20 min. + chilling
Cook: 10 min. + releasing
Makes: 3 servings

1⅓ cups heavy whipping
    cream
  3 large egg yolks
  ½ cup packed brown
    sugar
  ¼ tsp. ground cinnamon
  ½ tsp. maple flavoring
  1 cup water
TOPPING
  1½ tsp. sugar
  1½ tsp. brown sugar

TEST KITCHEN TIP
Make the desserts a day ahead. Simply top with sugar and caramelize right before serving.

1. Select saute setting on a 6-qt. electric pressure cooker and adjust for low heat. Add cream. Heat until bubbles form around sides of cooker. In a small bowl, whisk egg yolks, brown sugar and cinnamon. Select cancel setting; stir a small amount of hot cream into egg mixture. Return all to pressure cooker, stirring constantly. Stir in maple flavoring.

2. Transfer cream mixture to three greased 6-oz. ramekins or custard cups. Wipe pressure cooker clean. Pour in water; place trivet insert in bottom. Place ramekins on trivet, offset stacking as needed, and loosely cover with foil to prevent moisture from getting into ramekins. Lock lid; make sure vent is closed. Select manual setting; adjust pressure to high and set time for 10 minutes.

3. When finished cooking, allow pressure to naturally release for 10 minutes, then quick-release any remaining pressure according to manufacturer's directions. A knife inserted in the center should come out clean, though center will still be soft. Using tongs, remove ramekins. Cool for 10 minutes; refrigerate, covered, for at least 4 hours.

4. For topping, combine sugars and sprinkle over ramekins. Hold a kitchen torch about 2 in. above custard surface; rotate slowly until sugar is evenly caramelized. Serve immediately.

5. To brown under the broiler, preheat broiler and place ramekins on a baking sheet; let stand at room temperature for 15 minutes. Broil 8 in. from heat until sugar is caramelized, 3-5 minutes. Refrigerate until firm, 1-2 hours.

1 SERVING: 578 cal., 44g fat (26g sat. fat), 350mg chol., 63mg sod., 44g carb. (40g sugars, 0 fiber), 5g pro.

MOLTEN MOCHA CAKE

When I first made my decadent chocolate cake, my husband's and daughter's expressions said it all. Another time, I took the cake to our next-door neighbors. Their teenage son, who answered the door, ate the whole thing without telling anyone else about it!
—Aimee Fortney, Fairview, TN

Prep: 10 min.
Cook: 25 min. + releasing
Makes: 6 servings

1 cup water
4 large eggs
1½ cups sugar
½ cup butter, melted
1 Tbsp. vanilla extract
1 cup all-purpose flour
½ cup baking cocoa
1 Tbsp. instant coffee granules
¼ tsp. salt
Fresh raspberries or sliced fresh strawberries and vanilla ice cream, optional

1. Pour water into a 6-qt. electric pressure cooker. In a large bowl, beat eggs, sugar, butter and vanilla until blended. In another bowl, whisk flour, cocoa, coffee granules and salt; gradually beat into egg mixture.

2. Transfer to a greased 1½-qt. baking dish. Cover loosely with foil to prevent moisture from getting into dish. Place on a trivet with handles; lower into pressure cooker. Lock lid; make sure vent is closed. Select manual setting; adjust pressure to high and set time for 25 minutes.

3. When finished cooking, allow pressure to naturally release for 10 minutes, then quick-release any remaining pressure according to manufacturer's directions. A toothpick should come out with moist crumbs. If desired, serve warm cake with berries and ice cream.

1 SERVING: 723 cal., 29g fat (16g sat. fat), 247mg chol., 403mg sod., 107g carb. (76g sugars, 3g fiber), 12g pro.

TEST KITCHEN TIP
Make it a turtle cake by topping it with caramel and nuts.

APPLE COMFORT

When it's time for a warm, satisfying dessert, this heavenly apple crumble is my go-to specialty. It's ready in no time!
—Awynne Thurstenson, Siloam Springs, AR

Prep: 30 min.
Cook: 12 min. + releasing
Makes: 8 servings

- 1 **cup water**
- 6 **medium tart apples, peeled and sliced**
- 1 **cup sugar**
- ¼ **cup all-purpose flour**
- 2 **tsp. ground cinnamon**
- 2 **large eggs**
- 1 **cup heavy whipping cream**
- 1 **tsp. vanilla extract**
- 1 **cup graham cracker crumbs**
- ½ **cup chopped pecans**
- ¼ **cup butter, melted**
   Vanilla ice cream, optional

1. Add 1 cup water to a 6-qt. electric pressure cooker. In a large bowl, combine apples, sugar, flour and cinnamon. Spoon into a greased 1½-qt. souffle or round baking dish. In a small bowl, whisk eggs, cream and vanilla; pour over apple mixture. In another bowl, combine cracker crumbs, pecans and butter; sprinkle over top.

2. Loosely cover dish with foil to prevent moisture from getting into dish. Place on a trivet with handles; lower into pressure cooker. Lock lid; make sure vent is closed. Select manual setting; adjust pressure to high and set time for 12 minutes. When finished cooking, allow pressure to naturally release for 10 minutes, then quick-release any remaining pressure according to manufacturer's directions. Serve warm, with ice cream if desired.

1 SERVING: 433 cal., 24g fat (12g sat. fat), 96mg chol., 129mg sod., 53g carb. (40g sugars, 3g fiber), 5g pro.

TEST KITCHEN TIP
Be sure to choose an apple that holds up to pressure cooking. Granny Smith, Honeycrisp or Jonagold are all good options.

FLAN IN A JAR

Spoil yourself or the people you love with these delightful portable custards—a cute and fun take on the Mexican dessert classic. Tuck a jar into your lunch box for a sweet treat.
—Megumi Garcia, Milwaukee, WI

Prep: 25 min. + cooling
Cook: 6 min. + releasing
Makes: 6 servings

½ cup sugar
1 Tbsp. plus 1 cup hot water
1 cup coconut milk or whole milk
⅓ cup whole milk
⅓ cup sweetened condensed milk
2 large eggs plus 1 large egg yolk, lightly beaten
Dash salt
1 tsp. vanilla extract
1 tsp. dark rum, optional

1. In a small heavy saucepan, spread sugar; cook, without stirring, over medium-low heat until it begins to melt. Gently drag melted sugar to center of pan so sugar melts evenly. Cook, stirring constantly, until melted sugar turns a deep amber color, about 2 minutes. Immediately remove from heat and carefully stir in 1 Tbsp. hot water. Quickly pour into six hot 4-oz. jars.

2. In a small saucepan, heat coconut milk and whole milk until bubbles form around sides of pan; remove from heat. In a large bowl, whisk condensed milk, eggs, egg yolk and salt until blended but not foamy. Slowly stir in hot milk; stir in vanilla and, if desired, rum. Strain through a fine sieve. Pour egg mixture into prepared jars. Center lids on jars; screw on bands until fingertip tight.

3. Add remaining hot water to 6-qt. electric pressure cooker and place trivet insert in the bottom. Place jars on trivet, offset-stacking as needed. Lock lid; make sure vent is closed. Select manual setting; adjust pressure to high and set time for 6 minutes.

4. When finished cooking, allow pressure to naturally release for 10 minutes, then quick-release any remaining pressure according to manufacturer's directions. Cool jars 30 minutes at room temperature. Refrigerate until cold, about 1 hour. Run a knife around the sides of the jars; invert flans onto dessert plates.

1 FLAN: 223 cal., 10g fat (8g sat. fat), 100mg chol., 306mg sod., 28g carb. (27g sugars, 0 fiber), 5g pro.

BLACK & BLUE COBBLER

It never occurred to me that I could bake a cobbler in any device but my oven until I saw some other recipes and decided to experiment with my favorite dessert. It took a while to get right, but the tasty result was well worth it.
—Martha Creveling, Orlando, FL

Prep: 15 min.
Cook: 15 min. + releasing
Makes: 6 servings

1¾ cup water, divided
1 cup all-purpose flour
1½ cups sugar, divided
1 tsp. baking powder
¼ tsp. salt
¼ tsp. ground cinnamon
¼ tsp. ground nutmeg
2 large eggs, lightly beaten
2 Tbsp. whole milk
2 Tbsp. canola oil
2 cups fresh or frozen blackberries
2 cups fresh or frozen blueberries
1 tsp. grated orange zest
Whipped cream or vanilla ice cream, optional

1. In an 8-qt. electric pressure cooker, add 1 cup of water.

2. In a large bowl, combine the flour, ¾ cup sugar, baking powder, salt, cinnamon and nutmeg. Combine the eggs, milk and oil; stir into dry ingredients just until moistened. Spread the batter evenly onto the bottom of a greased 1½-qt. souffle or round baking dish.

3. In a large saucepan, combine the berries, remaining water, orange zest and remaining sugar; bring to a boil. Remove from the heat; immediately pour over batter. Place a piece of aluminum foil loosely on top to prevent moisture from getting into dish; place on a trivet with handles; lower into pressure cooker. Lock lid; make sure vent is closed. Select manual setting; adjust pressure to high and set time for 15 minutes. When finished cooking, allow pressure to naturally release for 10 minutes and then quick-release any remaining pressure according to manufacturer's instructions.

4. Uncover and let stand for 30 minutes before serving. Serve with whipped cream or ice cream if desired.

1 SERVING: 391 cal., 7g fat (1g sat. fat), 72mg chol., 190mg sod., 80g carb. (58g sugars, 4g fiber), 5g pro.

SERVE IT ON THE SIDE

While your entree simmers in the pot, whip up one of these easy add-ons. Made in the oven, in your slow cooker or on the stovetop, they'll round out all your meals deliciously.

BEANS, BACON & TOMATO BAKE

When I need a hearty side, I pull out the bacon, tomatoes and lima beans for a veggie-packed dish that satisfies everyone.
—Karen Kumpulainen, Forest City, NC

Prep: 10 min.
Bake: 35 min.
Makes: 12 servings

- 8 bacon strips, cut into 1-in. pieces
- 1 cup finely chopped onion
- ⅔ cup finely chopped celery
- ½ cup finely chopped green pepper
- 2 garlic cloves, minced
- 2 tsp. all-purpose flour
- 2 tsp. sugar
- 2 tsp. salt
- ¼ tsp. pepper
- 2 cans (14½ oz. each) diced tomatoes, undrained
- 8 cups frozen lima beans (about 42 oz.), thawed

1. Preheat oven to 325°. In a 6-qt. stockpot, cook bacon, onion, celery and green pepper over medium heat until bacon is crisp and vegetables are tender. Add garlic; cook 1 minute longer. Stir in flour, sugar, salt and pepper. Add tomatoes. Bring to a boil, stirring constantly; cook and stir 1-2 minutes or until thickened. Stir in beans.

2. Transfer to a greased 3-qt. baking dish or a 13x9-in. baking pan. Bake, covered, 35-40 minutes or until beans are tender.

⅔ CUP: 230 cal., 8g fat (3g sat. fat), 12mg chol., 666mg sod., 30g carb. (6g sugars, 9g fiber), 11g pro. **DIABETIC EXCHANGES:** 2 starch, 1½ fat.

TEST KITCHEN TIP
Spice things up by stirring a dash of crushed red pepper flakes or hot pepper sauce into the bean mixture. You can also dress it up a bit by topping the dish with a sprinkle of cheddar cheese immediately before serving.

JALAPENO-POPPER MEXICAN STREET CORN

Fresh sweet corn is always a hit, and this recipe is a definite standout. We love its creamy dressing, crunchy panko coating and spicy jalapeno kick. If you're really feeling wild, sprinkle these with a bit of cooked and crumbled bacon!
—Crystal Schlueter, Babbitt, MN

Takes: 30 min.
Makes: 4 servings

- 4 **ears fresh sweet corn**
- 2 **jalapeno peppers**
- 3 **Tbsp. canola oil, divided**
- ¾ **tsp. salt, divided**
- ¼ **cup panko (Japanese) bread crumbs**
- ½ **tsp. smoked paprika**
- ½ **tsp. dried Mexican oregano**
- 4 **oz. cream cheese, softened**
- ¼ **cup media crema table cream or sour cream thinned with 1 tsp. 2% milk**
- 2 **Tbsp. lime juice**
  Ground chipotle pepper or chili powder
  Chopped fresh cilantro, optional

1. Husk corn. Rub corn and jalapenos with 2 Tbsp. canola oil. Grill, covered, on a greased grill rack over medium-high direct heat until lightly charred on all sides, 10-12 minutes. Remove from heat. When jalapenos are cool enough to handle, remove skin, seeds and membranes; chop finely. Set aside.

2. Sprinkle corn with ½ tsp. salt. In a small skillet, heat remaining oil over medium heat. Add panko; cook and stir until starting to brown. Add paprika and oregano; cook until crumbs are toasted and fragrant.

3. Meanwhile, combine cream cheese, crema, lime juice and remaining salt; spread over corn. Sprinkle with bread crumbs, jalapenos, chipotle powder and, if desired, cilantro.:

NOTE: This recipe was tested with Nestlé crema; look for it in the international foods section.

1 EAR OF CORN: 339 cal., 26g fat (9g sat. fat), 39mg chol., 568mg sod., 25g carb. (8g sugars, 3g fiber), 6g pro.

EDAMAME SALAD WITH SESAME GINGER DRESSING

This bright salad has a little bit of everything: hearty greens, a nutty crunch, citrusy goodness and a big protein punch. It's pure bliss in a bowl.
—Darla Andrews, Schertz, TX

Takes: 15 min.
Makes: 6 servings

- 6 cups baby kale salad blend (about 5 oz.)
- 1 can (15 oz.) garbanzo beans or chickpeas, rinsed and drained
- 2 cups frozen shelled edamame (about 10 oz.), thawed
- 3 clementines, peeled and segmented
- 1 cup fresh bean sprouts
- ½ cup salted peanuts
- 2 green onions, diagonally sliced
- ½ cup sesame ginger salad dressing

Divide salad blend among six bowls. Top with all remaining ingredients except salad dressing. Serve with dressing.

1 SERVING: 317 cal., 17g fat (2g sat. fat), 0 chol., 355mg sod., 32g carb. (14g sugars, 8g fiber), 13g pro.

DID YOU KNOW?
Vitamin C-rich clementines help your body absorb iron from plant sources like the kale and edamame found in this salad. What a bonus!

FLAMBOYANT FLAMENCO SUMMER SALAD

I came up with this salad simply by choosing the best-looking vegetables at a local farmers market—the colors are so beautiful! Turn it into a full vegetarian entree by adding roasted chickpeas or cooked white beans.
—Crystal Schlueter, Babbitt, MN

Takes: 25 min.
Makes: 8 servings

- 3 medium rainbow carrots
- 4 medium blood oranges, peeled and segmented
- ½ small red onion, thinly sliced
- ½ medium fresh beet, thinly sliced
- ½ medium watermelon radish, thinly sliced
- 2 radishes, thinly sliced
- 2 Tbsp. chopped pistachios, toasted
- 2 Tbsp. chopped oil-packed sun-dried tomatoes
- 1 Tbsp. capers, drained
- ¼ tsp. salt
- ¼ tsp. pepper
- ¼ cup white balsamic vinaigrette
- 4 cups torn leaf lettuce
- ¼ cup shaved Manchego or Parmesan cheese

Using a vegetable peeler, shave carrots lengthwise into very thin slices; place in a large bowl. Add oranges, red onion, beet, radishes, pistachios, tomatoes, capers, salt and pepper. Drizzle with dressing; lightly toss to coat. Arrange lettuce on a platter; top with vegetable mixture. Top with cheese.

1 CUP: 103 cal., 6g fat (1g sat. fat), 4mg chol., 203mg sod., 12g carb. (8g sugars, 3g fiber), 2g pro. **DIABETIC EXCHANGES:** 1 vegetable, 1 fat, ½ fruit.

DID YOU KNOW?
Manchego cheese is a hard Spanish cheese made of sheep's milk. It offers a buttery texture and distinctively tangy flavor. You can replace it in most recipes with Parmesan or Asiago cheese.

PECAN BACON

Crispy, sweet bacon dresses up any breakfast menu. When my girls see this, they call it "special breakfast." The big flavor punch may just surprise you.
—Catherine Goza, Charlotte, NC

Prep: 10 min.
Bake: 30 min.
Makes: 6 servings

- 12 **bacon strips**
- ¼ **cup packed brown sugar**
- ¼ **cup finely chopped pecans**
- ⅛ **tsp. ground cinnamon**
- ⅛ **tsp. pepper**

1. Preheat oven to 375°. Place bacon in a single layer in a foil-lined 15x10x1-in. baking pan. Bake until lightly browned, 16-18 minutes.

2. Remove bacon from pan. Discard drippings from pan, wiping clean if necessary.

3. In a shallow bowl, mix remaining ingredients. Dip both sides of bacon in brown sugar mixture, patting to help coating adhere; return to pan.

4. Bake 8-10 minutes longer or until caramelized. Remove immediately from pan.

2 BACON STRIPS: 283 cal., 25g fat (8g sat. fat), 37mg chol., 373mg sod., 8g carb. (7g sugars, 0 fiber), 7g pro.

JALAPENO & COTIJA CHEESE POTATO STACK PIE

Pie isn't just for dessert anymore! Stacking thinly sliced potatoes with layers of minced jalapenos and crumbled cotija cheese helps turn ordinary potatoes into something truly spectacular...especially when served with salsa and sour cream.
—Colleen Delawder, Herndon, VA

Prep: 20 min.
Bake: 50 min.
Makes: 8 servings

2½ lbs. red potatoes, peeled and thinly sliced
¼ cup butter, melted
½ tsp. salt
¼ tsp. pepper
2 jalapeno peppers, seeded and minced
1¼ cups crumbled cotija cheese or crumbled feta cheese
Salsa and sour cream, optional

1. Preheat oven to 375°. Line a 15x10x1-in. pan with parchment paper. Remove the bottom of a 9-in. springform pan and place the round outer edge in the middle of the parchment paper.

2. Place the potatoes, butter, salt and pepper in a large bowl; toss to coat. Layer ⅓ of the potatoes evenly within the springform ring. Sprinkle with ⅓ of the jalapenos and ⅓ of the cheese. Repeat layers. Top with remaining potatoes and jalapenos.

3. Bake for 35 minutes. Top with remaining cheese. Bake 15-20 minutes longer or until potatoes are tender. Let stand 5 minutes before removing ring. Serve with salsa and sour cream, if desired.

1 SERVING: 223 cal., 12g fat (7g sat. fat), 34mg chol., 477mg sod., 23g carb. (2g sugars, 3g fiber), 7g pro.

CAULIFLOWER MASH

This quick and easy mashed cauliflower is a great alternative to same-old mashed spuds, and it's healthier, too!
—Nick Iverson, Denver, CO

Takes: 20 min.
Makes: 6 servings

- 1 **large head cauliflower, chopped (about 6 cups)**
- ½ **cup chicken broth**
- 2 **garlic cloves, crushed**
- 1 **tsp. whole peppercorns**
- 1 **bay leaf**
- ½ **tsp. salt**

1. Place cauliflower in a large saucepan; add water to cover. Bring to a boil. Reduce heat. Simmer, covered, until tender, 10-12 minutes. Drain; return to pan.

2. Meanwhile, combine remaining ingredients in a small saucepan. Bring to a boil. Immediately remove from heat and strain, discarding garlic, peppercorns and bay leaf. Add broth to cauliflower. Mash until reaching desired consistency.

1 SERVING: 26 cal., 0 fat (0 sat. fat), 0 chol., 308mg sod., 5g carb. (2g sugars, 2g fiber), 2g pro. **DIABETIC EXCHANGES:** 1 vegetable.

TEST KITCHEN TIP
When purchasing fresh cauliflower, look for a head with compact florets that are free from yellow or brown spots. The leaves should be crisp and green, not withered or discolored.

CRISPY BAKED ZUCCHINI FRIES

I coat zucchini strips with a mixture of panko bread crumbs, Parmesan cheese and spices, then bake them until they're crispy and golden brown. Delicious!
—Matthew Hass, Franklin, WI

Prep: 25 min.
Bake: 20 min.
Makes: 4 servings

- 2 **medium zucchini**
- 1 **cup panko (Japanese) bread crumbs**
- ¾ **cup grated Parmesan cheese**
- 2 **tsp. smoked paprika**
- ½ **tsp. garlic powder**
- ¼ **tsp. ground chipotle pepper**
- ¼ **tsp. salt**
- ¼ **tsp. pepper**
- ⅓ **cup all-purpose flour**
- 2 **large eggs, beaten**
- 3 **Tbsp. olive oil**

1. Preheat oven to 425°. Cut each zucchini in half lengthwise and then in half crosswise. Cut each piece lengthwise into ¼-in. slices.

2. In a shallow bowl, mix bread crumbs, cheese and seasonings. Place flour and eggs in separate shallow bowls. Dip zucchini slices in flour, egg and then in crumb mixture, patting to help coating adhere. Place on a greased rack in a foil-lined rimmed baking pan. Drizzle with oil. Bake until golden brown, 20-25 minutes.

1 SERVING: 289 cal., 18g fat (5g sat. fat), 106mg chol., 510mg sod., 21g carb. (3g sugars, 2g fiber), 12g pro.

EDDIE'S FAVORITE FIESTA CORN

When sweet corn is available, I love making this splurge of a side dish. Frozen corn works, but taste as you go and add sugar if needed.
—Anthony Bolton, Bellevue, NE

Prep: 15 min.
Cook: 25 min.
Makes: 8 servings

½ lb. bacon strips, chopped
5 cups fresh or frozen super sweet corn
1 medium sweet red pepper, finely chopped
1 medium sweet yellow pepper, finely chopped
1 pkg. (8 oz.) reduced-fat cream cheese
½ cup half-and-half cream
1 can (4 oz.) chopped green chilies, optional
2 tsp. sugar
1 tsp. pepper
¼ tsp. salt

1. In a 6-qt. stockpot, cook bacon over medium heat until crisp, stirring occasionally. Remove with a slotted spoon; drain on paper towels. Discard drippings, reserving 1 Tbsp. in pan.

2. Add corn, red pepper and yellow pepper to drippings; cook and stir over medium-high heat 5-6 minutes or until tender. Stir in remaining ingredients until blended; bring to a boil. Reduce heat; simmer, covered, 8-10 minutes or until mixture is thickened.

⅔ **CUP:** 249 cal., 14g fat (7g sat. fat), 39mg chol., 399mg sod., 22g carb. (9g sugars, 2g fiber), 10g pro.

HONEY-BUTTER PEAS & CARROTS

The classic combination of peas and carrots is made even better with a few simple flavor enhancers. Slow cooking allows the ingredients to meld for maximum richness.
—Theresa Kreyche, Tustin, CA

Prep: 15 min.
Cook: 5¼ hours
Makes: 12 servings

  1 lb. carrots, sliced
  1 large onion, chopped
  ¼ cup water
  ¼ cup butter, cubed
  ¼ cup honey
  4 garlic cloves, minced
  1 tsp. salt
  1 tsp. dried marjoram
  ⅛ tsp. white pepper
  1 pkg. (16 oz.) frozen peas

In a 3-qt. slow cooker, combine the first nine ingredients. Cook, covered, on low 5 hours. Stir in peas. Cook, covered, on high 15-25 minutes longer or until vegetables are tender.

½ **CUP:** 106 cal., 4g fat (2g sat. fat), 10mg chol., 293mg sod., 16g carb. (10g sugars, 3g fiber), 3g pro. **DIABETIC EXCHANGES:** 1 starch, 1 fat.

WHY YOU'LL LOVE IT...

"So easy! I opted to used fresh cracked black pepper instead of the white as that's what I had on hand."
—JMARTINELLI13, TASTEOFHOME.COM

PARMESAN ROASTED BROCCOLI

Sure, it's simple and healthy but, oh, is this roasted broccoli delicious. Cutting the stalks into tall trees turns this ordinary veggie into a standout side dish.
—Holly Sander, Lake Mary, FL

Takes: 30 min.
Makes: 4 servings

- 2 **small broccoli crowns (about 8 oz. each)**
- 3 **Tbsp. olive oil**
- ½ **tsp. salt**
- ½ **tsp. pepper**
- ¼ **tsp. crushed red pepper flakes**
- 4 **garlic cloves, thinly sliced**
- 2 **Tbsp. grated Parmesan cheese**
- 1 **tsp. grated lemon zest**

1. Preheat oven to 425°. Cut broccoli crowns into quarters from top to bottom. Place in a parchment paper-lined 15x10x1-in. pan. Drizzle with oil; sprinkle with seasonings.

2. Roast until crisp-tender, 10-12 minutes. Sprinkle with garlic; roast 5 minutes. Sprinkle with cheese; roast until cheese is melted and stalks of broccoli are tender, 2-4 minutes more. Sprinkle with lemon zest.

2 BROCCOLI PIECES: 144 cal., 11g fat (2g sat. fat), 2mg chol., 378mg sod., 9g carb. (2g sugars, 3g fiber), 4g pro. **DIABETIC EXCHANGES:** 2 fat, 1 vegetable.

PARMESAN SNAP PEA PASTA

My family loves pasta, so this simple dish is always a hit! Not only does the recipe come together easily, but it makes a lot so it's perfect for potlucks.
—Crystal Jo Bruns, Iliff, CO

Takes: 30 min.
Makes: 12 servings

- 1 **lb. fresh sugar snap peas (about 5 cups), trimmed**
- 1 **pkg. (16 oz.) angel hair pasta**
- 5 **Tbsp. olive oil, divided**
- 1 **medium red onion, finely chopped**
- 3 **garlic cloves, minced**
- ½ **tsp. salt**
- ¼ **tsp. crushed red pepper flakes**
- ⅛ **tsp. coarsely ground pepper**
- 1¼ **cups grated Parmesan cheese, divided**

1. In a 6-qt. stockpot, bring 16 cups water to a boil. Add peas; cook, uncovered, just until crisp-tender, 3-4 minutes. Using a strainer, remove peas from pot.

2. In same pot, add pasta to boiling water; cook according to package directions. Drain, reserving 1 cup cooking water; return to pot. Toss with 3 Tbsp. oil.

3. In a large skillet, heat remaining oil over medium heat; saute onion until tender, 2-3 minutes. Add garlic and seasonings; cook and stir 1 minute. Stir in peas; heat through.

4. Toss with pasta, adding 1 cup cheese and reserved cooking water as desired. Sprinkle with remaining cheese.

¾ **CUP:** 258 cal., 9g fat (2g sat. fat), 7mg chol., 254mg sod., 35g carb. (4g sugars, 3g fiber), 10g pro.

THE BREAD BASKET

Few things complete menus like golden, aromatic breads fresh from the oven. Let this chapter of bonus recipes make mealtime memorable in your home.

VEGGIE CORN MUFFINS

These muffins go with so many main courses. We love to add healthy ingredients to all our recipes. I welcome the challenge, and it's something my family appreciates.
—Peggie Brott, CO Springs, CO

Takes: 30 min.
Makes: 1 dozen

- 1 **cup yellow cornmeal**
- ½ **cup all-purpose flour**
- ½ **cup whole wheat flour**
- 1 **tsp. baking powder**
- ¾ **tsp. salt**
- 1 **large egg**
- 1 **cup unsweetened almond milk**
- ¼ **cup canola oil**
- ¼ **cup honey**
- ½ **cup finely shredded carrot**
- ½ **cup finely chopped green pepper**

1. Preheat oven to 400°. Coat 12 muffin cups with cooking spray.

2. Whisk together the cornmeal, flours, baking powder and salt. In another bowl, whisk together egg, milk, oil and honey. Add to cornmeal mixture; stir just until moistened. Fold in the vegetables. Fill prepared cups two-thirds full.

3. Bake until a toothpick inserted in center comes out clean, 12-15 minutes. Cool 5 minutes before removing from pan to a wire rack. Serve warm.

FREEZE OPTION: Freeze cooled muffins in resealable plastic freezer bags. To use, microwave each muffin on high until warmed, 30-45 seconds.

1 MUFFIN: 159 cal., 6g fat (1g sat. fat), 16mg chol., 207mg sod., 25g carb. (6g sugars, 2g fiber), 3g pro. **DIABETIC EXCHANGES:** 1½ starch, 1 fat.

ZUCCHINI & CHEESE DROP BISCUITS

My colorful little drop biscuits are very easy to put together and yet are packed with flavor. I serve them warm out of the oven. What a tasty way to use zucchini!
—Keith Mesch, Mount Healthy, OH

Prep: 25 min. + standing
Bake: 25 min.
Makes: 1 dozen

¾ cup shredded zucchini
1¼ tsp. salt, divided
2½ cups all-purpose flour
1 Tbsp. baking powder
½ cup cold butter, cubed
½ cup shredded cheddar cheese
¼ cup shredded part-skim mozzarella cheese
¼ cup shredded Parmesan cheese
2 Tbsp. finely chopped oil-packed sun-dried tomatoes, patted dry
2 Tbsp. minced fresh basil or 2 tsp. dried basil
1 cup 2% milk

1. Preheat oven to 425°. Place zucchini in a colander over a plate; sprinkle with ¼ tsp. salt and toss. Let stand 10 minutes. Rinse and drain well. Squeeze zucchini to remove excess liquid. Pat dry.

2. In a large bowl, whisk flour, baking powder and remaining salt. Cut in butter until mixture resembles coarse crumbs. Stir in zucchini, cheeses, tomatoes and basil. Add milk; stir just until moistened.

3. Drop by scant ⅓ cupfuls into a greased 13x9-in. baking pan. Bake 22-26 minutes or until golden brown. Serve warm.

1 BISCUIT: 205 cal., 11g fat (7g sat. fat), 29mg chol., 482mg sod., 22g carb. (2g sugars, 1g fiber), 6g pro.

WHY YOU'LL LOVE IT...

"I have made these biscuits multiple times for a variety of occasions. Each time they are received very well. At my house, they're part of breakfast buffets and served with hot soups."

—CHEMMAGIC, TASTEOFHOME.COM

APRICOT-ROSEMARY SCONES

Pair these easy sweet-savory scones with a comforting bowl of soup or colorful entree salad. Making them is much easier than you might think.
—Charlene Chambers, Ormond Beach, FL

Prep: 25 min.
Bake: 15 min.
Makes: 16 scones

- 4 cups all-purpose flour
- 2 Tbsp. sugar
- 2 Tbsp. baking powder
- ¾ tsp. salt
- 1½ cups cold butter, cubed
- 1 cup chopped dried apricots
- 1 Tbsp. minced fresh rosemary
- 4 large eggs, lightly beaten
- 1 cup cold heavy whipping cream

TOPPING
- 1 large egg, lightly beaten
- 2 Tbsp. 2% milk
- 2 tsp. sugar

1. Preheat oven to 400°. Whisk together flour, sugar, baking powder and salt. Cut in cold butter until the size of peas. Stir in apricots and rosemary.

2. In a separate bowl, whisk eggs and whipping cream until blended. Stir into flour-butter mixture just until moistened.

3. Turn onto a well-floured surface. Roll dough into a 10-in. square. Cut into four squares; cut each square into four triangles. Place on baking sheets lined with parchment paper.

4. For topping, combine egg and milk. Brush tops of scones with egg mixture; sprinkle with sugar. Bake until golden brown, 12-15 minutes.

FREEZE OPTION: Freeze cooled scones in resealable plastic freezer bags. Reheat in a preheated 350° oven 20-25 minutes, adding time as necessary to heat through.

1 SCONE: 372 cal., 25g fat (15g sat. fat), 121mg chol., 461mg sod., 32g carb. (7g sugars, 1g fiber), 6g pro.

GARLIC ASIAGO BREAD

Folks always rave about this recipe. It has chunks of cheese and fabulous garlic taste. We have bread sales at our school for fundraisers, and this is always one of the top sellers.
—Charlotte Thomas, Pollock Pines, CA

Prep: 30 min. + rising
Bake: 20 min. + cooling
Makes: 2 loaves
(10 wedges each)

- 1 pkg. (¼ oz.) active dry yeast
- 1¼ cups warm water (110° to 115°)
- 2 Tbsp. plus 2 tsp. olive oil
- 7 garlic cloves, minced
- 1 Tbsp. sugar
- 2 tsp. salt
- 1½ tsp. white vinegar
- 3 to 3¼ cups bread flour
- 1 cup cubed Asiago cheese

EGG WASH
- 1 large egg
- 1 Tbsp. water

1. In a large bowl, dissolve yeast in warm water. Add the oil, garlic, sugar, salt, vinegar and 2 cups flour. Beat until smooth. Stir in enough of the remaining flour to form a firm dough. Stir in cheese.

2. Turn onto a floured surface; knead until smooth and elastic, 6-8 minutes. Place in a greased bowl, turning once to grease the top. Cover and let rise in a warm place until doubled, about 1 hour.

3. Punch dough down; divide in half. Shape into 5-in.-round loaves. Place on lightly greased baking sheets. Cover and let rise in a warm place until doubled, about 30 minutes.

4. For egg wash, in a small bowl, combine egg and water. Brush over loaves. Bake at 375° for 20-25 minutes or until golden brown. Cool on wire racks.

1 WEDGE: 107 cal., 4g fat (1g sat. fat), 9mg chol., 254mg sod., 15g carb. (1g sugars, 1g fiber), 5g pro. **DIABETIC EXCHANGES:** 1 starch, ½ fat.

TEST KITCHEN TIP
Unopened packages of dry yeast should be stored in a cool, dark, dry place and used by the "best if used by" date on the package. Opened packages or bulk dry yeast should be stored in an airtight container in the refrigerator for about six weeks.

CHAPATI BREADS

My daughter and I make this Indian flatbread frequently. It's so fun and goes well with any spiced dish. We use the extras to make sandwich wraps.
—Joyce McCarthy, Sussex, WI

Prep: 20 min.
Cook: 5 min./batch
Makes: 10 servings

1½ cups all-purpose flour
½ cup whole wheat flour
1 tsp. salt
¼ tsp. garlic powder
¾ cup hot water (140°)
2 Tbsp. olive oil

1. In a large bowl, combine the flours, salt and garlic powder. Stir in water and oil. Turn onto a floured surface; knead 10-12 times. Divide dough into 10 portions. On a lightly floured surface, roll each portion into a 6-in. circle.

2. In a large nonstick skillet, cook breads over medium heat for 1 minute on each side or until lightly browned. Keep breads warm.

1 FLATBREAD: 113 cal., 3g fat (0 sat. fat), 0 chol., 237mg sod., 19g carb. (0 sugars, 1g fiber), 3g pro. **DIABETIC EXCHANGES:** 1 starch, ½ fat.

BEERNANA BREAD

It's simple arithmetic: Beer is good. Banana bread is good. Beernana bread is great! This recipe is a guaranteed crowd-pleaser. Even novices who don't know their way around the kitchen can pull this one off.
—Steve Cayford, Dubuque, IA

Prep: 15 min.
Bake: 55 min. + cooling
Makes: 1 loaf (16 slices)

- 3 cups self-rising flour
- ¾ cup quick-cooking oats
- ½ cup packed brown sugar
- 1½ cups mashed ripe bananas (about 3 medium)
- 1 bottle (12 oz.) wheat beer
- ¼ cup maple syrup
- 2 Tbsp. olive oil
- 1 Tbsp. sesame seeds
- ¼ tsp. kosher salt

1. Preheat oven to 375°. In a large bowl, mix flour, oats and brown sugar. In another bowl, mix bananas, beer and maple syrup until blended. Add to the flour mixture; stir just until moistened.

2. Transfer to a greased 9x5-in. loaf pan. Drizzle with oil; sprinkle with sesame seeds and salt. Bake 55-60 minutes or until a toothpick inserted in center comes out clean. Cool in pan 10 minutes before removing to wire rack to cool.

FREEZE OPTION: Securely wrap and freeze cooled loaf in foil and place in resealable plastic freezer bag. To use, thaw at room temperature.

1 SLICE: 173 cal., 2g fat (0 sat. fat), 0 chol., 304mg sod., 35g carb. (13g sugars, 1g fiber), 3g pro. **DIABETIC EXCHANGES:** 2 starch, ½ fat.

TEST KITCHEN TIP
When baking this bread, steer clear of the IPAs (India pale ales). They will likely give your bread a bitter flavor.

BEST-EVER CRESCENT ROLLS

My daughter and I have cranked out dozens of these homemade rolls. It's a real team effort. I cut the dough into pie-shaped wedges; she rolls them into crescents.
—Irene Yeh, Mequon, WI

Prep: 40 min. + chilling
Bake: 10 min./batch
Makes: 32 rolls

  3¾ to 4¼ cups all-purpose
    flour
  2 pkg. (¼ oz. each) active
    dry yeast
  1 tsp. salt
  1 cup whole milk
  ½ cup butter, cubed
  ¼ cup honey
  3 large egg yolks
  2 Tbsp. butter, melted

TEST KITCHEN TIP
Create chive crescents by dividing ⅔ cup minced fresh chives between the two circles of dough.

1. Combine 1½ cups flour, yeast and salt. In a small saucepan, heat milk, cubed butter and honey to 120°-130°. Add to dry ingredients; beat on medium speed 2 minutes. Add egg yolks; beat on high 2 minutes. Stir in enough remaining flour to form a soft dough (dough will be sticky).

2. Turn dough onto a floured surface; knead until smooth and elastic, about 6-8 minutes. Place in a greased bowl, turning once to grease the top. Cover with plastic wrap and let rise in a warm place until doubled, about 45 minutes.

3. Punch down dough; place in a resealable plastic bag. Seal and refrigerate overnight.

4. To bake, turn dough onto a lightly floured surface; divide in half. Roll each portion into a 14-in. circle; cut each circle into 16 wedges. Lightly brush wedges with melted butter. Roll up from wide ends, pinching pointed ends to seal. Place 2 in. apart on parchment paper-lined baking sheets, point side down. Cover with lightly greased plastic wrap; let rise in a warm place until doubled, about 45 minutes.

5. Preheat oven to 375°. Bake until rolls are golden brown, 9-11 minutes. Remove from pans to wire racks; serve warm.

FREEZE OPTION: Immediately after shaping, freeze rolls on parchment paper-lined baking sheets until firm. Transfer to a resealable plastic bag; return to freezer. Freeze up to 4 weeks. To use, let rolls rise and bake as directed, increasing rise time to 2½-3 hours.

1 ROLL: 104 cal., 4g fat (3g sat. fat), 28mg chol., 107mg sod., 14g carb. (3g sugars, 1g fiber), 2g pro.

FRY BREAD

Crispy, doughy and totally delicious, this fry bread is fantastic with nearly any sweet or savory toppings you can think of. Customize it to fit your main course. We love it on its own with a little butter, a drizzle of honey and a squeeze of lemon.
—Thelma Tyler, Dragoon, AZ

Prep: 20 min. + standing
Cook: 15 min.
Makes: 12 servings

  2 **cups unbleached flour**
  ½ **cup nonfat dry milk powder**
  3 **tsp. baking powder**
  ½ **tsp. salt**
4½ **tsp. shortening**
  ⅔ **to ¾ cup water**
     Oil for deep-fat frying
     Butter, honey and lemon juice, optional

1. Combine flour, dry milk powder, baking powder and salt; cut in shortening until crumbly. Add water gradually, mixing to form a firm ball. Divide dough; shape into 12 balls. Let stand, covered, for 10 minutes. Roll each ball into a 6-in. circle. With a sharp knife, cut a ½-in.-diameter hole in center of each circle.

2. In a large cast-iron skillet, heat oil over medium-high heat. Fry dough circles, one at a time, until puffed and golden, about 1 minute on each side. Drain on paper towels; if desired, serve warm with butter, honey and fresh lemon juice.

1 PIECE: 124 cal., 5g fat (1g sat. fat), 1mg chol., 234mg sod., 17g carb. (2g sugars, 1g fiber), 3g pro.

BEST DINNER ROLLS

If you can't decide which enticing topping to use, just make them all.
—Christina Pittman, Parkville, MO

Prep: 35 min. + rising
Bake: 10 min.
Makes: 2 dozen

- ¼ cup sugar
- 1 pkg. (¼ oz.) active dry yeast
- 1¼ tsp. salt
- 4½ to 5 cups all-purpose flour
- 1 cup whole milk
- ½ cup water
- 2 Tbsp. butter
- 2 large eggs
- 1 large egg, lightly beaten

FOR EVERYTHING DINNER ROLLS
- 1 tsp. kosher salt
- 1 tsp. dried minced garlic
- 1 tsp. dried minced onion
- 1 tsp. poppy seeds
- 1 tsp. sesame seeds

FOR PARM-GARLIC DINNER ROLLS
- 2 Tbsp. grated Parmesan cheese
- ½ tsp. dried minced garlic

FOR ALMOND HERB DINNER ROLLS
- 2 Tbsp. chopped sliced almonds
- ½ tsp. kosher salt
- ½ tsp. dried basil
- ½ tsp. dried oregano

1. In a large bowl, mix sugar, yeast, salt and 2 cups flour. In a small saucepan, heat milk, water and butter to 120°-130°. Add to dry ingredients; beat on medium speed 3 minutes. Add 2 eggs; beat on high 2 minutes. Stir in enough remaining flour to form a soft dough (dough will be sticky).

2. Turn dough onto a floured surface; knead until smooth and elastic, 6-8 minutes. Place in a greased bowl, turning once to grease the top. Cover with plastic wrap and let rise in a warm place until doubled, about 1 hour.

3. Punch down dough. Turn onto a lightly floured surface; divide and shape dough into 24 balls. Place in two greased 13x9-in. baking pans. Cover with kitchen towels; let rise in a warm place until doubled, about 30 minutes. Preheat oven to 375°.

4. Brush rolls with lightly beaten egg. Sprinkle with toppings for rolls of your choice. Bake 10-15 minutes or until golden brown. Remove from pans to wire racks; serve warm.

1 ROLL: 118 cal., 2g fat (1g sat. fat), 30mg chol., 143mg sod., 21g carb. (3g sugars, 1g fiber), 4g pro.

TEST KITCHEN TIP
You can easily turn the dough into twists. Start by making the dough as directed, and divide it into 24 portions. Shape into balls; roll each into a 10-in. rope. Fold rope in half and twist two or three times, holding both ends. Pinch rope ends to seal. Let rise; top and bake as directed.

MONKEY BREAD BISCUITS

My easy dinner biscuits, featuring garlic and Italian seasoning, are a savory take on the popular monkey bread treat. Your family will love them with any meal.
—Dana Johnson, Scottsdale, AZ

Takes: 20 min.
Makes: 1 dozen

- 1 **tube (16.3 oz.) large refrigerated flaky biscuits**
- 3 **Tbsp. butter, melted**
- 1 **garlic clove, minced**
- ½ **tsp. Italian seasoning**
- ¼ **cup grated Parmesan cheese**
  Additional Italian seasoning

1. Preheat oven to 425°. Separate biscuits; cut each into six pieces. In a large bowl, combine butter, garlic and Italian seasoning; add biscuit pieces and toss to coat.

2. Place four pieces in each of 12 greased muffin cups. Sprinkle with cheese and additional Italian seasoning. Bake 8-10 minutes or until golden brown. Serve warm.

1 BISCUIT: 159 cal., 9g fat (3g sat. fat), 9mg chol., 418mg sod., 16g carb. (3g sugars, 1g fiber), 3g pro.

WHY YOU'LL LOVE IT...

"I made these to go with soup for lunch. We all enjoyed them. They are fast, easy and good. Make quick work of cutting the biscuits by stacking two or three and then cutting them at once."
—BUFFETFAN, TASTEOFHOME.COM

INDEX